DALLAS:
CHASING THE URBAN DREAM

Akard Street view of the Adolphus Hotel *Daniel Barsotti*

DALLAS:
CHASING THE URBAN DREAM

BY PHILIP SEIB

With Photographs By Daniel Barsotti

P R E S S W O R K S
DALLAS, TEXAS

ACKNOWLEDGEMENTS

Many of the ideas I discuss in this book first saw light in my weekly column in *The Dallas Morning News*. To Burl Osborne, president and editor of the *News*, I owe my thanks for entrusting me with space on his op ed page and giving me free rein to address the issues I think important.

My editors at the *News*, Carolyn Barta and Rena Pederson, always have provided much encouragement and good advice. I thank them for their patience while I have plunged into various crusades.

Anne Dickson has proved through the work of Pressworks Publishing just how important small publishing houses continue to be. Anne's faith in and concern about Dallas made this book possible.

First Printing
1234567890

Library of Congress Catalog Card Number: 85-719-80
ISBN 0-939722-29-1

FOREWORD

Dallas. Its mention evokes a variety of images. Dallas Cowboys football. The comic venality of television's J.R. Ewing. An economic Shangri La impervious to the chill of recession.

A hundred years ago, Dallas was a city of 10,000 persons. Only fortuitous placement of railroad tracks guaranteed its survival. During this century, and particularly during the past decade, Dallas has flourished, becoming the quintessential modern boomtown.

Why? What lures wealth and stimulates growth? Dallas is not a pretty city. Neither natural nor man-made attractions measure up to those of many other American cities. There is, nevertheless, an abounding self-confidence, an esprit de la cite among its residents, and an absence of the despair that has crept into the lives of so many urban dwellers.

Dallas is doing something right. It can teach other cities some things about urban success, but it also offers some lessons in what *not* to do. On balance, Dallas at least begins to live up to one of the slogans that has been attached to it: "a city that works."

The problems Dallas faces are not unique. The city is troubled by widespread crime, inadequate transportation systems, ineffective schools, and a host of other major difficulties. For the most part, Dallas has shown a willingness to attack these problems aggressively.

Even in times of national economic slowdown,

Dallas voters have proved willing to pass massive bond propositions in support of everything from fire station construction to renovation of the state fairgrounds. In the midst of the 1982 recession, a $247 million bond package passed overwhelmingly. In 1981, when Dallas voters were presented a referendum on imposing a strict ceiling on taxes (modeled on California's Proposition 13), the measure was approved in only six of the city's 244 voting precincts.

This book addresses a number of the issues Dallas and most other major American cities face. I outline and comment on some of the measures Dallas has undertaken -- some successfully, others not. I hope the lessons of Dallas might prove instructive to other cities that will follow the same general course today or tomorrow.

In spite of the often discouraging experiences of many cities in recent years, Americans still cling to an urban dream -- an expectation that there always will be some green amidst the concrete, some music rising above the honking automobile horns, and some rays of sunshine piercing the smog.

Is this an unattainable dream or merely a dream deferred? We must assume it is the latter, because without the energy hope engenders, all would be lost. This residual optimism is a fundamental characteristic of Dallas. The city expects the urban dream to be fulfilled.

Philip Seib
1985

CONTENTS

Alley mural, Greenville Avenue *Daniel Barsotti*

I.

WATCHING THE CITY

You can hear Dallas growing. You are never far from the roar of earth-movers, the crackle of acetylene torches, and the whoosh of cement being mixed.

You can see the growth, too, particularly along the downtown skyline dotted with new towers and construction cranes. The once scattered stands of glass and steel are becoming forests.

For the city watcher, Dallas's exuberance is fascinating. Little self-doubt exists; only success is expected.

This attitude is, for the most part, healthy, but it tends to discourage introspection. Sometimes the rush to ever more growth seems too headlong. If Dallas lacks anything, it is the self-discipline required to stop and think.

Robust expansionism has become the trademark of Dallas. The growth doesn't stop, and barely slows, even while the nation weathers a recession. Envious eyes turn to Dallas in such times; other cities hope they are glimpsing their own futures.

This is the dynamic surface of Dallas as hustling boomtown. But other kinds of growth are underway.

Dallas's minority population is growing. Blacks and Mexican-Americans constitute almost half the Dallas citizenry, but leadership positions in government and business are filled almost exclusively by Anglos.

Demands for social services are growing faster than local government is willing or able to respond. Inadequate public housing and health care, for example, periodically generate public protests and news media attention, which in turn elicit short-term remedial measures from city hall. This stopgap approach is as old-fashioned as the physical growth of the city is modern.

And although Dallas's surface shines ever more brightly as it grows, parts of the city's infrastructure are shrinking.

The public education system endures a permanent state of siege as costs lengthen their lead over funding and as more Anglo parents pull their children out of the Dallas Independent School District. Some public schools in affluent North Dallas have been closed because of low enrollment, while schools in minority neighborhoods are overcrowded.

Although the Anglo student population dropped by 50 percent between 1970 and 1980, in the mid-1980s some hope appeared. The school year beginning in August, 1984, marked the second consecutive year of rising Anglo enrollment. Tough-minded reforms in the classroom and aggressive public relations efforts had their desired effect: parents became willing to give the DISD another chance.

Another kind of shrinkage Dallas faces is that which plagues every major American city — flight to the suburbs by homeowners and businesses.

Such an exodus destroys a city's tax base, exacerbating problems of paying for social services and creating a difficult-to-reverse flow of development capital away from the city. A constant struggle must be waged to maintain the city's attractiveness in the face of seductive "come hither" advances from the suburbs.

Although these attacks on the city's health are common throughout urban America, Dallas's counterpunching is uncommonly aggressive. Some older cities have achieved remarkable results in what largely have been reclamation projects that salvage decayed areas (such as Baltimore's waterfront). Dallas has been trying to stay ahead of the game.

For example, the new downtown arts district is being created at the same time the northern edge of downtown is being developed. Thus, the amenities that often are introduced to try to save an area are being born here at the outset. The new sector of downtown will grow around the arts district, and if the district draws its expected visitors and generates its anticipated level of activity, this part of downtown might never need rescuing.

The glitter of urban affluence is made more attractive by its rarity in American cities. Success, particularly when made manifest in shiny new construction, can be hypnotic.

If you visit downtown Dallas, you will find yourself surrounded by the marvels of skyscraper construction: the mine-like pit dug for the foundation of a 70-story building; the daring construction workers on skeletons of steel that reach into the clouds; the parade of girders and glass climbing the sides of the new structure.

This is particularly dramatic if you keep in your mind's eye a chain of time-lapse pictures of the Dallas skyline. The city of just 15 years ago, rising from the flat Texas landscape, was dominated by the Mobil Building's red neon Pegasus and punctuated by an occasional office tower. As the years have passed, the pictures have changed, becoming crowded with an increasingly dense and ever more lofty array of buildings.

Today, Pegasus and those first towers are hard to find; they are dwarfed by newcomers. You can still see gaps in the skyline, but nothing is more certain than that they soon will be filled.

Watching Dallas grow is a fine spectator sport, but most persons view the continuing spectacle with studied nonchalance. After all, the unspoken reasoning seems to be, "This is Dallas and therefore there is nothing unusual about such growth and success."

This attitude borders on smugness and flirts with the inherent dangers of self-satisfaction.

The city's life proceeds on its own for the most part. Occasional bond issues or referenda attract some attention. The news media do a fairly good job of covering the day-to-day business of local government. Cheerful good faith is the dominant, if sometimes not wholly realistic, attitude about how the city is being run.

This faith usually is not abused. Dallas city hall is efficient and generally responsive. The business community maintains a close dialogue with elected officials. The private sector constantly suggests new development plans; city officials have to worry little about prodding business to pay attention to the growth of the city.

For example, a private architectural firm came up with the idea for a "Water Walk" through part of downtown. In addition to stimulating commercial development along this promenade, the in-town park would bring a needed amenity to the largely arid city.

This would be a true joint venture: city land and private capital, with both sides involved in planning the project.

Part of the confidence in the way the city is being run stems from the fiscal health of the community, from city government to new entrepreneurial ventures. This is an important way in which Dallas differs from many other major American cities.

Watching most cities can be dispiriting. New York's much-publicized "bankruptcy" was not an anomaly. The lethal combination of shrinking tax base, rising costs, elevated citizen expectations, and inadequate long-range planning will virtually guarantee financial disaster. These ingredients are present to some degree in most communities.

Dallas so far has dodged most of these bullets

through a combination of good sense and good luck. The city will continue to need ample portions of both.

Staunching the flow of homeowners to the suburbs has been one of Dallas's achievements. Middle- and upper-class residential neighborhoods close to downtown continue to grow.

The grand neighborhoods of early Dallas once seemed doomed to being replaced by cheap apartment houses and commercial development, but many of these old homes are being saved and restored; their value is rapidly appreciating. In some other neighborhoods, where older houses were beyond rescue and had turned into unsavory rental properties, new condominium projects have been created to attract young professionals who want to live close to downtown offices.

In addition to supporting the theory that the city is inhabitable, this residential development makes more secure the city's tax base. Property tax revenues from inner city residential real estate are *increasing*. In many cities, this is unheard of.

This slowdown of residential flight hasn't come about entirely by accident. To encourage a town house and condominium development at the edge of downtown, the city council authorized a buy-back guarantee to the property's developer.

The buy-back safeguard wasn't needed. The project, Bryan Place, turned out to be enormously successful and is expanding.

Bryan Place is within walking distance of most of downtown. Within a few minutes of this project are other new residential areas featuring condominiums for sale beginning at about $75,000. The price range is great: a restored house on Swiss Avenue can command a half million dollars, and 60-year old bungalows nearby are selling for $140,000 (up 100 percent during the past six years).

This prosperity is by no means uniform throughout the city. As you wander through different parts of town, you will find the Dallas mystique strengthened in some areas, foreign in others. Such a journey is instructive even for a long-time resident. You can discover many Dallases.

In the midst of the resurgent in-town neighborhoods are the enclave cities of Highland Park and University Park, with their fastidiously groomed houses of many members of the Dallas elite, their own ubiquitous police forces, and excellent (and de facto segregated) public schools.

The secure isolation of these Park Cities once was envied with some bitterness by nearby Dallas residents. That has diminished; these homeowners no longer consider themselves "have nots." As property values have risen (especially in Lakewood to the east and Oak Lawn to the west of the Park Cities), residential growth has spawned compatible commercial development — neighborhood stores and restaurants that are patronized with a joyous possessiveness by nearby residents.

If you move farther from downtown in concentric circles, to the north you will find affluence increasingly common. Homes become newer and more lavish. Commercial development — principally retail stores — also is new and like the homes in the area thrives on land that few decades ago was farmed.

Away from North and parts of East Dallas (and a few scattered areas elsewhere), the glitter fades. To see these parts of the city realistically, you must take care to not become mesmerized by the lustre and hype of the self-generated and self-perpetuated Dallas legend. Not all is affluence; not all is perfection.

To move south from downtown is to step back in time. South Dallas is largely black, shunned by new businesses and seen by many Dallasites as a blemish on their prosperous city and thus best ignored. The wealth and upward mobility of the northern part of the city are unknown here. South Dallas is more concerned with survival than with growth.

Periodically emerging from City Hall are ambitious plans for reshaping the economy of South Dallas. Most private developers, however, resist suggestions to look south. The momentum is in North Dallas; projects there tend to be instant goldmines. Why take the many risks that would be part of resuscitating another part of town?

Southwest of downtown, racially-mixed Oak Cliff constantly vies with the city center "north of the Trinity River" and tries (with some recent success) to share in renovation and growth.

Farther west is yet another neglected area, home for many blacks and Mexican-Americans. This part of town also has yet to participate in the city's growth; it is largely a dependency, waiting for whatever aid programs government can send its way.

To the southeast of downtown, Pleasant Grove has a solid, mostly Anglo residential base. It, too, is growing, but its conservative, working class character is changing little.

Given the disparities within the city, how will Dallas try to share its wealth and erase at least the most glaring inequities in the city's life?

For all its strengths, Dallas has been remarkably hesitant in its approach to comprehensive planning, particularly when addressing problems of the economically weak parts of the city.

No one can look at Dallas without being impressed with its achievements to date, but nor can anyone fail to wonder how the growth can be maintained and expanded.

Momentum is largely an illusion; some refinements are necessary even in policies that have had the cumulative success of those under which Dallas has thrived.

Long-range planning is inherently conservative. If plans are followed, flexibility will be controlled. Persons who have made fortunes by taking advantage of flexibility in matters such as zoning are naturally reluctant to accept limits on their options.

Much of the debate about planning centers on the nebulous topic of "the quality of life." The general character of a city's life is important, but the phrase itself principally serves those who delight in high-sounding rhetoric. The main issue remains that of protecting the tax base and marshalling resources in order to provide basic services. Without strength in this matter, "the quality of life" is certain to suffer.

What spurs a homeowner to leave the city? Perhaps

it is because he can't get his garbage picked up regularly or he can't count on an ambulance arriving promptly in an emergency. Perhaps cheaper housing and better schools make the suburbs irresistible. What would chase a business owner to the suburbs? Perhaps his utility rates are perpetually skyrocketing or maybe traffic congestion near his office keeps customers away.

These aren't cosmic issues, but they are sufficiently frightening to city officials who worry about where the tax revenues will come from ten years from now. An impetus for planning, therefore, is simply the recognition that residents (businesspeople and homeowners) need assurance that they won't be subjected to undue economic or social trauma.

When put in these terms, little opposition to planning appears. But when city hall tries to alter zoning in an area or suggests changes in density and transportation patterns, resistance emerges promptly.

Dallas has yet to make up its mind about planning. But it is naive to assume the city's good fortune will continue indefinitely and it is hypocritical to expect that the benefits engendered by a well-managed growing city should be accompanied by a laissez-faire governance.

City watchers carry with them their own crystal balls and enjoy contemplating the urban future. In Dallas, the present casts its image forward, encouraging optimistic predictions. If the vision of today's downtown skyline appears in the crystal, the seer can feel sanguine. But below the skyline there remain fundamental issues that cannot be avoided forever.

Disparities among sections of the city have to be at least partially reduced. Downtown has yet to prove it can attract residential development and nightlife or even maintain its traditional retail businesses. Growth has avoided logical patterns. That cannot continue indefinitely; there simply isn't room for helter-skelter development. The march towards gridlock must be halted; the newly born Dallas Area Rapid Transit system *must* work.

Just as Dallas's current strength rests in large part on the willingness of government, business, and individual citizens to *attack* problems, so too the future will depend on the energies devoted to finding realistic answers to new and continuing problems.

The mood of Dallas has been shaped and toughened through self-reliance. No one awaits windfalls of federal or state aid. Foreign investors are welcome, but their presence is not considered crucial. The personalities and ideologies of national and state politicians are considered to be of little consequence.

The spirit of Dallas is not fueled by money alone. The religious community is huge. In this Baptist heartland (where the First Baptist Church can boast a congregation of more than 25,000 members), Methodist, Presbyterian, Episcopalian and other denominations and religions play a major role in community life.

Occasionally, religious leaders directly intervene in city politics, such as in 1985, when the president of the Greater Dallas Community of Churches addressed the city council to chastise a council member for racist comments.

Usually, however, church influence is more subtle. Clergy and lay leaders regularly sit around the luncheon tables in Dallas's elite private clubs to discuss city issues. Through these meetings as well as via messages from the pulpit, the religious community helps focus attention on social issues.

The city's spirit also finds inspiration of a more secular kind in the exploits of local sports teams. The Dallas Cowboys long have been (for good or ill) a symbol of Dallas. By 1984, however, the expansion professional basketball team, the Mavericks, threatened to outdo the Cowboys in inspiring fans' zealousness. College and high school sports also have large numbers of rabid fans.

Even ex-jocks wield influence in Dallas. Former Cowboy star Roger Staubach retired to become — what else — a real estate developer. Former college football hero Bob Folsom became first a real estate developer and then mayor of the city.

Such links illustrate how diverse paths through the city's life often eventually converge.

Dallas continues to derive much of its strength from its insular nature. Just as the city withstood the vicissitudes of the turgid national economy of the early 1980s, so too do city leaders anticipate being able to weather future national economic or political turbulence.

This might seem a relatively defensive posture, but most people in Dallas appear quite comfortable with it. The sense of security born of this self-sufficiency (or at least the illusion of such) helps foster dreams of what Dallas might yet be.

Thanksgiving Square *Daniel Barsotti*

II
GOVERNING THE CITY

Dallas is big and rich and growing in a way that assuredly will make it bigger and richer. A city's grand size and wealth, however, do not ensure its effective governance.

The new Dallas City Hall is an appropriate physical representation of the Dallas style of government. Walking through the flashily elegant, I.M. Pei-designed building, you will find everything in remarkably good order. Nowhere to be seen are the cigar-chomping pols who dominate politics in other cities. One wonders where the secret, smoke-filled rooms might be.

A stroll through city hall, with its open offices and glass walls, is like wandering through a governmental aquarium. Everything is happening before your eyes: the computers spew out tax notices; the city council holds forth in its plush auditorium; and meetings of a seemingly infinite number of boards, commissions, and committees are always in progress.

Dallas is the largest city in America to use the council-manager form of government. The elected mayor and city council members serve on a part-time basis for which they are paid $50 per meeting. For many council members this "part-time" job consumes about 60 hours each week.

Day-to-day responsibility for city operations rests with the city manager, a professional administrator hired by the council and paid about $95,000 per year to run a bureaucracy of almost 14,000 employees.

Voters select the council members, who in turn make fundamental policy choices, and then the manager and his staff implement those policies. Of course, if any one of the elements of this process breaks down, the entire system is jeopardized. The city manager tends to keep things moving, even when the council, for whatever reason, is not providing guidance. This leads to occasional charges that the manager is totally running the city, even though he is unelected.

Advocates of pure democracy might criticize the power of the city manager, but more pragmatic observers find much to praise in this system. Efficient administration usually is not impeded by politics. Chicago-style patronage and partisanship are virtually unheard of in the Dallas system, except when council members make appointments to city boards and commissions.

The city manager is responsible for every municipal function, from trash pick-up to long-range land use planning. Because of Dallas's status as the premier council-manager city, the manager is able to recruit the emerging stars of public administration from throughout the nation for his staff. The system usually hums along smoothly.

From time to time, the insular quality of this management process creates problems. For example, the manager and his staff might be working on a comprehensive thoroughfare plan but might fail to stay in touch with neighborhood organizations in areas that would be affected by such a plan. Because political pressure on the manager comes only indirectly — from voters via their elected council members — the professional administrators sometimes are accused of insensitivity and of attempting to foist insufficiently debated policies upon the city.

Avoiding such problems requires constant contact between manager and council. A clear mark of any city manager's maturing in this job is his increasing sensitivity to the political pressures integral to the survival of the city's elected officials. A thin line exists between the pristine avoidance of politics and irresponsible isolation. Sometimes a city manager finds it difficult to avoid crossing that line.

In theory, the manager cannot act by fiat; the council must approve or reject his recommendations. But on a daily basis, it is the manager who is on the job full time. He does not have to run to the council about minor administrative matters. Another fine line exists here: when does a minor administrative matter become a substantive policy question meriting council action? This line sometimes is invisible.

A typical city council agenda illustrates how the division of power works. The agenda includes a list of several dozen items such as zoning changes and contract approvals that require council action. The council usually acts based on a briefing by the city staff. Unless a council member on his own or through his constituents has been alerted to additional elements of the issue, the staff presentation is likely to substantially determine the council's position. Also, local news media play watchdog roles, at times stimulating council activity on issues.

This process has worked well. Little corruption or severe incompetence has appeared among city staff, and most city business is transacted with a valid assumption of good faith.

Planning might seem an inescapable part of governing the modern city, but it is such a difficult and controversial task (with few immediate rewards) that some cities perpetually postpone it. The result can be chaos. A classic example that Dallas residents enjoy pointing to with horror is Houston's failure to enact zoning ordinances during that city's greatest bursts of growth.

The spectre of Houston certainly should haunt Dallas because Dallas seems likely to fall into some of the same traps that have caused Houston's insufferable congestion.

A comprehensive plan and a zoning-change moratorium for Far North Dallas once were proposed by the city planning department. Angry developers mustered their political clout and convinced the city council to reject the plan. Development of this part of town then proceeded at breakneck speed. Massive shopping malls, hotels, and office complexes were erected on roadways wholly inadequate to meet the sudden influx of traffic.

Major developers reaped healthy profits, but unplanned growth in North Dallas far outstripped available services. By 1983, Dallas and suburban cities affected by rapid growth were searching for funds for highway improvements and for some logical consistency in the development pattern that would allow projections of what the future might hold.

Many kinds of planning are needed: transportation and land use planning are among the "umbrella" categories. Not only must different types of planning be undertaken, but they all must be coordinated. For example, by late 1982 Dallas city hall finally was concentrating more on the linkage between transit and the density of commercial and residential development.

The political cost of planning is high. Some developers and some homeowners almost certainly will see their interests infringed upon as part of the price for what might be undefined "improvements" in an unpredictable future.

Dallas, like other cities, must resist the seductive attractiveness of plunging ahead without comprehensive planning. The temptation is great to mortgage the future if doing so will enhance the present.

Dallas has become notorious as a graveyard for plans and planners. On numerous occasions, when planners' and developers' ideas have collided, the developers' influence with the city council has prevailed. The plans and the planners disappeared.

Prior to 1984, the city council refused to approve

any comprehensive land use plan. Persons opposed to these plans — principally developers and support industries that would profit from unrestrained development — could wield enough influence among council members to kill restrictive planning. This influence was the product of well-placed campaign contributions and non-stop jawboning.

By 1984, the city's politics had changed. Homeowners had organized even in traditionally tranquil North Dallas. Council members saw that planning might be a determinative issue on election day. The council, after various compromises, approved the city manager's new planning policies that most notably tied development limits to the traffic problems any project would create.

Part of the Dallas planning process fosters intense politicking. A 15-person City Plan Commission is appointed by the city council. The commission must judge all requests for zoning changes and recommendations made by the professional planning staff. After consideration by the commission, the council votes on the matter, sometimes being presented with a recommendation by the plan commission and a contrary recommendation from the planning staff. The council usually follows the commission's recommendations.

A preliminary step toward planning that requires careful consideration is establishing a basic agenda. Just what in the city needs long-term planning? What aspects of today's city even will exist ten or twenty years from now, and what should they then be like?

These questions might sound vague, but such is the

nature of initiating long-range planning for a city. Not only must this needs assessment be comprehensive, but it also must be politically palatable. This means developing a "democratic" process to solicit the public's suggestions and thus win the popular support necessary to sustain the process. This kind of democracy can prove unmanageable and in the long run do little to aid planning.

The "Dallas 2000" project was designed specifically to meet such needs. Orchestrated by the city's planning department, "Dallas 2000" solicited participation by neighborhood activists. Task force meetings and plenary sessions debated growth patterns, housing, transportation, neighborhood preservation, education, and other issues. Of course, with so many vested interests represented in the meetings, it often was hard to cut through the self-serving rhetoric and to develop substantive positions.

Among the most intriguing of the "Dallas 2000" tools were maps designed to show development trends and predictions of land use changes and rates of growth throughout the city. These maps immediately became controversial.

If, for example, the map indicated a particular area in which "some deterioration is expected," residents of that area would become enraged, demanding the designation be changed to reflect a more optimistic prognosis.

Reality rarely entered into such debates; the map might have been totally accurate in its identification of the city's "soft spots," but politics and chauvinism can overwhelm honesty.

For example, when maps labeled parts of South Dallas (those with mainly black residents) as facing continuing deterioration, the debate quickly became one about alleged racism rather than development potential.

City council members were asked to participate actively in the "Dallas 2000" planning sessions, and the council as a whole was expected to rally behind the project as the principal guidepost for an official city planning policy.

This didn't happen. Perhaps council members were worried about the political heat the meetings generated or maybe they just had other things to do, but they were noticeably absent from the "2000" meetings and likewise were unenthusiastic in their comments about the project.

Although "Dallas 2000" was not the great popular triumph its designers had wanted, it did stimulate widespread recognition that planning is essential. This in itself was a giant step for the city. Using the consciousness created by "Dallas 2000," city officials (particularly the city manager and his staff) encouraged continuing discussion of planning options.

By late 1982, Dallas planners began to raise new issues. Principal among these is "density."

The density debate in Dallas is about an issue that is beyond discussion in many cities. In New York City it long has been accepted that because of the scarcity (and thus expense) of land, housing and office space must be stacked high, making maximum use of every available square foot of land.

Dallas, however, always has built most of its city on

a low density basis. For example, in 1982 there were only about a dozen high-rise apartment houses in the entire city. In the center of downtown, office skyscrapers arise whenever land becomes available, but this concentrated development has been the exception rather than the rule in Dallas.

Single-family housing on ample lots reaches into downtown, a rarity in any city of almost one million inhabitants. As the city continues to grow, something has to give.

Considerable growth (both residential and commercial) is taking place in Dallas suburbs such as Irving, where Las Colinas, a planned business and residential community expecting 120,000 residents, is rising from the prairie.

Dallas also has seen tremendous growth of its apartment complexes, mostly two- or three-story buildings (some with thousands of units per complex) spread over what not long ago was farmland in North Dallas. Also becoming popular by late 1982 were small, simple, single-family homes built on smaller than normal lots and selling at moderate prices.

What Dallas has *not* seen, however, is widespread construction of high-rise residential buildings, not even close to downtown or on major transportation routes (with the exception of several luxury buildings on Northwest Highway in near North Dallas and on Turtle Creek in close-to-downtown Oak Lawn). Outside the central business district, Dallas zoning has emphasized height restrictions, set-backs, and other limitations that give much of Dallas (again, even close to downtown) a sprawling look that is more suburban than urban.

For most persons living in Dallas, this has been a luxurious growth pattern. At least until recently, much open space existed in the city. This is part of the legacy of the Dallas of the 1870s, when the city's population barely topped 3,000.

From 3,000 to 900,000 in a century, even with expanded city boundaries, means that land becomes precious. Some Dallas residents argue, "Let's keep our low density pattern and let the overflow move to the suburbs." That sounds good until you ponder Dallas's most pressing issue of the 1980s — transportation.

The transit battle in Dallas has run the gamut of issues from debates about the best people-moving technology to political wheeling and dealing. Even when most Dallasites admit that the city needs a realistic mass transit system, many of these same people refuse to acknowledge the changes such a system necessarily will make in the look of the city.

City planners face this lack of realism when they try to sell the idea that land use and transit planning cannot be considered separately, but have to be recognized as being mutually dependent.

Mass transit cannot be ubiquitous; principal routes run through certain clearly defined corridors. Passengers must get to those corridors, and this in turn requires additional transportation, either by private automobile or a web of bus "feeder" routes. Obviously, the mass transit problem is simplified if as many of the system's passengers as possible live near the principal corridors. This would require in those areas a residential density that Dallas so far has not accepted.

To foster a logical plan of increased residential density, the plan commission and city council are offering some developers zoning allowances if they include residential components in their projects. For instance, a proposed building might be allowed 20 stories and reduced set-back requirements if it includes some residential space, but only 12 stories and stricter set-back guidelines if only commercial space is built. (This incentive approach is being tried first in Oak Lawn.)

The generic kinds of North American city are the deconcentrated (spread out), such as Dallas has been so far, and the concentrated, such as New York. Problems plague both these models: the first tends to be inefficient, with overspending (on a per capita basis) on roads, utility lines, and whatever else needs to reach everyone; the second often becomes overcrowded.

A happy medium might exist. The great opportunity Dallas planners have between now and the end of this century is to define what kind of city will exist as the twenty-first century begins. For instance, can Dallas become more realistically concentrated without suffering the pains of overcrowding?

The planning process designed to develop this Dallas of the future, according to the city manager, will address the following issues: transportation, "hard" services (such as sewer, water, energy), "soft" services (such as schools, police, health), and open space (parks). These must be considered both separately and jointly.

However creative the design of the planning

process and whatever the extent of public participation, the process is only as good as the results it delivers. And this is what Dallas claims to specialize in —making the city work.

An attribute of government that Dallas prizes is the extensive cooperation between the standard institutions of government and the highly involved local business community.

Some persons allege that these are indistinguishable and that Dallas government really is merely an appendage of the city's business interests. That thesis is an oversimplification. A partnership based on shared interests does function, but pursuit of common goals does not necessarily mean that invidious hidden agendas exist.

The business-government linkage usually is unostentatious. A good example of this is the work of the Central Dallas Association, an organization of 170 members, mostly representatives of banks, large retailers, insurance companies, and other businesses. Founded in 1958, the CDA is funded entirely by its members; it receives no financial support from government.

The organization does, however, engage in a variety of quasi-governmental activities, some of which it conducts and funds jointly with the city government. Projects include studies of downtown parking needs, walkway and streetscape plans, and historic preservation policy-making.

The CDA also is active in local political affairs, generally following City Hall's lead in support of bond issues and other referenda and serving as a communications channel to the approximately 140,000 persons who work downtown.

City Hall is not bashful about asking for CDA or other private sector involvement in planning or other activities. Potential conflicts of interest generally are ignored; the shared goals of continued growth, expanded job opportunities, and increased financial rewards serve as motivation for these joint endeavors.

This process represents marvelous cooperation or insidious elitism, depending on the eye of the beholder. Whatever the observer's opinion, this approach undoubtedly epitomizes much of the governing process of Dallas today.

No magic endows Dallas with greater administrative efficiency than that of other cities. The ability to deliver services has been carefully nurtured. In most instances, the city government has not allowed significant gaps between demand for services and the ability to meet those demands. Dallas, therefore, has not been forced to play "catch up," which always is an expensive game.

Part of maintaining a city is keeping track of what is going on — what streets need repairs, what water mains are due for replacement, how many service trucks are on duty, and so forth. This is not a matter of magic, but merely of organization. Computers track the city's needs and responses to those needs. By keeping backlog low, responsiveness can be prompt, particularly in emergencies.

Good city services mean property values increase, which in turn means the tax base remains healthy enough to fund the services.

When the average citizen thinks about how well his government is working, he is unlikely to ponder philosophies of governance or spend much time thinking about what the city will be like in the next century.

Was his garbage picked up this week? How long did it take to get his street's potholes filled? Is police protection adequate? Are there parks nearby? Are museums and cultural activities easily accessible? Those probably are the important issues.

Recent elections in Dallas seem to indicate general satisfaction with the political status quo. Since 1979, Dallas voters have rejected only one referendum or bond proposal that was backed by the "establishment." That was the 1981 transit election, a remarkably poorly run campaign. Since then, another transit issue, in 1983, passed by a large margin.

If there is a flaw in Dallas's governance, it arises in nagging questions about who is represented. Although Dallas's population is approximately 29 percent black and 14 percent Hispanic, minority group clout at City Hall usually is negligible.

The traditional reasons create this problem, such as ineffective political organization in the minority communities, and factional battling within those communities. Many minority voters have become so accustomed to receiving minimal attention that they have lost their interest in the city's governmental processes.

This underrepresentation exacerbates the racial tensions that rarely become visible but nevertheless exist in Dallas. Minority community spokesmen have called for redesigning the city council, by adding seats or by replacing at least two of the three at-large seats with additional single-member districts. So far, the council has refused to do this.

The single-member versus at-large debate illustrates some prevalent attitudes about government in Dallas. The at-large seats (one of which is the mayor's) are defended with the argument that it remains possible for a council member to represent "all of Dallas."

Not surprisingly, these at-large seats usually are held by residents of affluent, vote-heavy North Dallas. Even though their intentions are good, these council members are unlikely to be fully sensitive to needs of neighborhoods that are socio-economically different from their own.

The lesson Dallas has yet to fully learn about its governance is that efficiency and representativeness are not necessarily the same thing. Although the former characteristic is evident throughout the city, the latter remains elusive.

Trinity Church *Daniel Barsotti*

III

NEIGHBORHOODS AND TRANSIENCE

In trying to envision "the city," we easily can forget that the urban whole is merely the sum of its parts. Each of a city's constituent elements may have its own character, which in turn helps shape the character of the entire city.

Among these facets of a city's life are its neighborhoods, steadfast islands in the unruly stream of daily events.

The amorphous geography of the city, with new development popping up willy-nilly, can be disorienting. Where is home? Is it merely at a given intersection, within one of the look-alike apartment complexes? The neighborhood is something more than this; it is a physical entity to which we may cling. In our neighborhood, we know where we are.

Most of us who grew up in a large city or even in a small town remember a distinct geographical area that was our own. We enjoyed the characteristics that gave our neighborhood its insular quality. We were from a neighborhood, as well as from a city or state. If we moved, we would return to the old neighborhood for visits even while we were building new loyalties to a new home.

This was an integral part of American urban life. But today is the neighborhood an anachronism? Is the idea of neighborhood obsolete? Some persons say that with our mobility an entire city is our neighborhood and that the spirit of neighborhoods breeds a balkanizing competition, stunting development of the community as a whole.

Giving weight to this argument for the end of neighborhoods, particularly in a city such as Dallas, is the transience of so much of the population. Large parts of Dallas are covered with massive apartment complexes, homes for people who eschew ties, who plan to live in one place for about a year and then move to a suburb or some more distant place.

The vast size of the "baby boom" generation has forced significant changes in the delivery of services in America. As members of this generation come of age, they have been slow to develop roots and have embraced a lifestyle shaped in youth perhaps by crowded classrooms and then continued in crowded apartment complexes. Higher divorce rates, lower birth rates, and the growing tendency to move quickly from job to job all diminish ties to "home."

Mobility encourages transience, which in turn discourages loyalty to neighborhood (until, and if, roots begin to develop). For city planners, this absence of loyalties can be useful; planning can proceed in a vacuum since a transient population is unlikely to care enough to fight for an area they are just passing through.

Who, after all, will fight against rezoning the land where this year's apartment stands? Who cares if three years from now that land is covered by an office tower?

But many people in Dallas are resisting the tides of transience. Dallas is seeing a rebirth of neighborhood loyalties and neighborhood issues are being debated with increasing frequency.

In the early 1970s, Dallas seemed likely to follow in the wake of other cities, with increasing flight to the suburbs leaving in-town residential neighborhoods to lower income groups or to the wrecking ball. Homes that were showplaces of Dallas when they were built 50 years ago were rapidly becoming slums.

When prospects for these homes seemed to have reached their nadir, a stunning reversal occurred. One neighborhood's residents secured a historic district designation for their houses. This blocked developers, who might have simply torn down the old houses, and led to loan and tax incentives for persons who restored residences within the neighborhood.

This Swiss Avenue district attracted residents who were able to buy the houses at relatively low prices (often because of their neglected condition) and who promptly spent money and enormous effort to renovate them. While this was going on, other older neighborhoods — even those not receiving the official "historic" designation — were being similarly resuscitated.

Many persons doing this were young couples who liked the idea of being close to their downtown offices and who didn't want to face increasingly frustrating traffic problems that plague commuters from the suburbs. As these "urban pioneers" plowed their money into their homes, they became increasingly possessive of their neighborhoods, monitoring city hall decisions about land use and traffic planning.

Homeowners soon found allies among proprietors of businesses small enough to consider themselves "neighborhood" establishments. These businesspeople recognized the value of the stability inherent in neighborhoods with active, protective residents.

Development of this pro-neighborhood constituency has not been universally welcomed. City hall officials who like to create policies that are applicable city-wide find aggravating those neighborhood residents who argue that their needs are special and do not conform to a generic approach that can be applied across the board to the entire city.

A homogeneous city might be easier to govern than is a melange of interests, but such expedience fosters drabness. The diversity of neighborhoods makes the city a sampler, offering varied environments for varied tastes. That encourages in-town, rather than suburban, living.

Neighborhoods also have varied needs that place demands on municipal services. For example, a single-family home on a large lot will require different utility capabilities than would an apartment house on that same lot. A neighborhood of single-family homes might want traffic controls (stop signs, low speed limit) to protect the quiet of the area, but a planner looking at the city's overall transportation needs might prefer a larger, higher-speed thoroughfare.

By the start of the 1983 mayoral campaign, the future of neighborhoods had become a major political issue in Dallas. Neighborhood activists recognized a basic rule of politics: the wheel that squeaks the loudest gets the grease. "Homeowners' rights" became a principal topic for candidates' debates.

Political activism isn't easy. As one pro-neighborhood businesswoman notes, "It takes a Herculean effort to band together, first to understand how the city is manipulating your neighborhood and then to do something about it." Many neighborhood residents, however, realize they have no choice but to pursue this activist course.

Organizational efforts within a neighborhood follow a certain pattern. There is the first, tentative get-together in a borrowed church or school auditorium, often spurred by a zoning case or crime problems. Usually, an air of urgency pervades the meeting. Sometimes a veteran organizer from another neighborhood will make a guest appearance. He or she will discuss everything from drafting bylaws to lobbying the city council.

The people at these meetings quickly lose their neophyte status. They plunge into matters such as deciding whether renters should be given voting rights in the organization equal to those of homeowners. They discuss building a communications network within the neighborhood and decide what they want to do — everything from an anti-burglary program to a neighborhood picnic.

Throughout these discussions, one theme quietly dominates: By articulating their wants and needs, these residents are redefining "neighborhood."

Zoning and thoroughfare plans attract the most attention from neighborhood groups when they monitor city hall. But in many cases the issue that first stimulates neighborhood organization is crime.

During the 1970s, when Dallas — like many other cities — felt the bite of rising crime rates, the police department encouraged neighborhood "crime watch" programs to increase citizens' awareness of what is going on around them. These projects are basically "buddy systems" in which neighbors keep an eye on each other's homes and promptly report suspicious activity to the police.

Less simple, however, is the organizational discipline of a crime watch. This requires that neighbors know each other and that an effective communication system exist within the neighborhood. As these facets of the crime watch program are put in place, goals often expand. The neighbors who started talking with each other about crime soon start discussing traffic, neighborhood beautification, and other issues.

As with the crime watch, the issue remains self-protection, but protection extending to long-term property values.

Crime watches in Dallas have helped control burglary rates. They also have stimulated more sophisticated neighborhood organization. The first tentative meetings are often followed by politically charged gatherings at which candidates for office try to woo an increasingly knowledgeable electorate.

These politicians soon learn few issues are as hot as a perceived threat to property values. They also soon recognize that few persons are more likely to vote than the homeowner who sees his or her property values endangered.

Dallas's city government professionals — the bureaucrats who don't have to face the voters — only gradually have come to understand the significance of these neighborhood organizations. This tardiness makes little sense, since property value protectionism works to the advantage of the city government. The higher the appraised values of the homes, the greater the tax revenues to the city.

City hall has been slow to recognize that these homeowners will put up with only so much — their commitment to the city is not so irrevocable that they might not simply pick up and head for the suburbs if they believe the city government consistently will be unresponsive to their interests.

This schism between the city's government and some of its residents has affected the tone of Dallas politics. In a city where rough-and-tumble political fighting is both rare and implicitly discouraged, neighborhood leaders have let it be known that they will not play by the old rules. They appear en masse at city council meetings and take hours of the council's time to state (and restate) their opinions.

However belatedly, city hall has moved away from its earlier philosophy of, "Let's not be distracted from the issue of the future of *all* of Dallas by becoming caught up in neighborhood concerns." The response to this from the neighborhoods was, "Without us, what is the city?"

This dispute has to be resolved; both sides are too potent to allow lingering confrontation. A logical vehicle for rapprochement could be the city council since all the neighborhoods are represented (with varying degrees of diligence) by these elected officials. Some of the council members, however, have been reluctant to work with competing factions within their own districts. These politicians see no need to risk generating more fights they would have to referee.

An alternative force for reconciliation could be to create a Neighborhoods Council. The city council would divide (more or less arbitrarily) the city into neighborhoods from which representatives would gather to hammer out issues positions for consideration by the council.

An immediate problem with this is the unwieldy nature of such an apparatus. By late 1982, the Dallas City Manager's office had a directory (admittedly incomplete) of almost 200 neighborhood organizations. Some of these groups included several hundred activists, while others were composed of a dozen lethargic residents. Pulling these disparate organizations together probably would create an entertaining, but ineffective, body.

Some council members make it a point to hold "town hall" meetings in various neighborhoods within their districts and similarly try to attend neighborhood organizations' gatherings. This provides an informal link to city hall that varies in effectiveness according to the dedication of individual council members. City officials seem satisfied with this unstructured approach. With the growing political clout of neighborhood organizations and their increased involvement in city issues, such informality might not suffice much longer.

The greatest danger of an informal approach to neighborhood interests is the ease with which irrevocable decisions can be made without neighborhood participation. Several Dallas neighborhoods — some purely residential, others mixed-use — underwent zoning modifications that encourage high-rise development. Little if any public discussion of these matters took place; the procedure was out of the sight of any but the most diligent citizens who took the trouble to haunt numerous city hall meeting rooms. After being presented with faits accomplis, some Dallas residents screamed that they had been duped. But this was too little, too late.

In response to such outcry, the city went out of its way to include neighborhood residents and business owners in planning the future of Oak Lawn, a mixed-use area near downtown. The city even hired a planning consultant to participate in establishing the land use strategy.

Oak Lawn undeniably is heading for all the riches and troubles of a boom. Its proximity to downtown makes it attractive for high density residential and office development. Its streets are woefully inadequate; unrestrained growth in the area assuredly would lead to gridlock.

As the Oak Lawn planning sessions progressed,

participants succeeded not only in devising a rational development scheme, but also in forging a cooperative working relationship between residents and developers.

This diminution of antipathy between these groups could pave the way for similar efforts in other parts of town. In Oak Lawn, a popular bumper sticker had read, "Save Oak Lawn; Shoot a Developer." If such hostility could be calmed here, it probably can be stilled elsewhere as well.

Part of the tension between homeowners and developers is a product of political paranoia (no evidence of coordinated developers' conspiracies to bamboozle homeowners has been uncovered), but the realities of competing interests make it only natural that these two groups should watch each other warily.

If residents did not take time to present their cases to the politicians (and to the news media), prospects for developer dominance at city hall would be much greater. The political naivete that would allow this imbalance is now a thing of the past.

During the 1985 campaigns for mayor and council, seeking the "homeowner vote" was an integral part of the electoral strategy of every serious candidate. Because Dallas's municipal elections are nonpartisan, candidates must find alternatives to party organizations to generate voter turnout. If there is conflict between homeowners and developers, the homeowners have the edge. The developer can contribute money to a candidate, but rarely can he directly affect voter turn-out. Organized homeowners have the strength of numbers.

Homeowner clout has reached into statewide races also. For example, during the 1982 campaign for governor, some East Dallas homeowners asked incumbent Bill Clements and challenger Mark White about Dallas transportation issues of particular concern to several neighborhoods. White's response was considered most acceptable, so some of the area homeowners wrote an endorsement letter and hand-distributed it to thousands of homes in East Dallas. The letter touted White (and several other candidates) as "pro-neighborhood" and thereby deserving voter support. White and the other persons endorsed did exceptionally well in the areas where this letter was circulated.

Only after several elections will it be possible to precisely gauge the electoral significance of neighborhood organizations. They are, however, clearly filling a vacuum as Dallas politics becomes more competitive and sophisticated. If the political clout of these groups grows, the elected officials whose political fortunes depend on the neighborhood organizations will find additional ways to formally include neighborhood interests in the planning process.

Does this presage "balkanization" of the city? Perhaps not. "Pluralism" (a more congenial term) is inevitable in an urban political environment in which no powerful, centralized political machines exist. If the city government makes reasonable efforts to ensure that neighborhood interests are heard and legitimate concerns draw appropriate responses, cutthroat competition among the different parts of the city can be avoided.

Rather than foster divisiveness, renewed interest in neighborhoods might turn out to be a constructive manifestation of nostalgia. A restoration of values as well as of buildings could evolve if homeowners and businesspeople maintain their commitments to preserving the identity of neighborhoods.

Traditional neighborhood life is a counterpoint to the ever-diminishing "personality" of the American city. Stark contrasts abound, as on the Dallas street where an old house stands, still salvageable, next to a lot where a like structure has been razed and a defiantly ugly apartment house has arisen in its place.

Perhaps this is inexorable evolution, required by urban growth, that strips away the clutter of character and leaves us with streamlined, efficient blandness. Or perhaps this evolution need not be so sweeping; maybe we can selectively retain elements of the past without surrendering prospects for the future.

This, then, is the fundamental question about the future of neighborhoods: Is character in a city worth saving? In Dallas, the answer is a tentative "Yes."

Fair Park *Daniel Barsotti*

IV

THE EDUCATION STRUGGLE

A Dallas schoolteacher recently asked an administrator: "I'm told to teach 12th graders 12th-grade material when they read at 5th-grade level. What am I supposed to do?" The administrator was unable to answer.

Both the question and the non-response are common in discussions about American education. Although much of the news about public education these days is dominated by the actions of politicians and judges, student incompetence looms as an inescapable, dark presence.

Dallas has undertaken the Sisyphus-like task of trying to save its public schools. The quest has been plagued by aggravation so constant that it threatens to doom the school system to permanent chaos.

Desegregation litigation begun in 1955 continues to drain the Dallas Independent School District's emotions and finances. Busing and other race-related adjustments have kept school administrators worrying more about courtrooms than about classrooms.

Many Anglo parents have responded by pulling their children out of DISD schools. Between 1970 and 1980, the DISD population dropped from 58.2 percent to 29.3 percent Anglo. During the same decade, while the school's tax base shrunk, the per pupil cost of running the schools climbed from $684 per year to $1873 per year.

Education became a cause celebre in the entire state in 1984 when a commission chaired by Dallas businessman H. Ross Perot called for drastic reforms in the academic regimen and fiscal base of the public school system. A special session of the Legislature enacted a tax increase to turn most of the Perot Commission's recommendations into actual policy.

While the state reforms took hold, voters in the Dallas Independent School District made a similar financial commitment when they approved $196 million for school construction and renovation in a 1985 bond election.

These turnaround measures came after years of neglect during which academic standards sagged and education policy became a punching bag for politicians.

Politics usually has victims. In this case, the victims were students whose educations limped along under burdens that have little to do with traditional elements of schooling.

The 1985 bond proposition passed by a 2-to-1 margin, winning in every section of the city. Bond supporters' ranks contained a "Who's Who" of the Dallas establishment. These leaders raised over $500,000 for the campaign and convinced voters that the election was not only to decide the future of decaying school buildings, but also was a referendum on the future of the city.

The theory cited in campaign literature and speeches was that no city's tax base can survive if the public school system is allowed to collapse. This was the argument that won support from voters who didn't have children in the DISD or other direct interest in the schools.

Voters' endorsement of the DISD proposition sent an important signal to the federal judges who have been directing and monitoring the school system's seemingly endless desegregation efforts. After years of bitterness caused by busing and court-imposed standards for personnel and classroom procedures, approval of the bond projects offered proof that Dallas was ready to get on with the task of educating its children.

The 1985 vote for upgrading schools throughout the district implicitly endorsed fairness and quality schooling in all DISD schools. That can be a rationale for withdrawal by the judges (who never have been enthusiastic about or skilled at shaping education policy.)

No single election, however, can "fix" the quality of education. Those of us who several decades ago graduated from big city public schools are bewildered by the demise of the schools. When we left elementary school, we could spell. Today, many college students have yet to master the skills we learned by age 12.

When we went to school, homework, attendance, and teachers were taken seriously. (When we watched movies such as "Blackboard Jungle," we considered them almost science fiction; today they might be viewed as documentaries.)

Within the schools, gradual improvements are taking place. DISD Superintendent Linus Wright slowly is reducing the number of administrators. This, in turn, should cut expenses and eliminate some of the paperwork that distracts teachers from their more important classroom tasks.

Education and bureaucracy often are not compatible. For example, why introduce another layer of administration to make up lesson plans, rather than leaving this as a responsibility for individual teachers? Setting teaching standards is fine, but this doesn't mean an administrator should dictate day-to-day teaching operations. Teachers understandably rebel against such insults to their competence and against the ridiculous waste of paying excess personnel to do unnecessary work.

Another reform enacted by the DISD board at Wright's recommendation is termination of "social promotion," the policy that advanced students from grade to grade regardless of their performance. Moving bodies through the system is fine if your only goal is to avoid overcrowded classrooms, but too many graduates of such a process are likely to be lazy and stupid.

Social promotion epitomizes the decline of our schools. It is a classic example of putting logistics and bureaucracy ahead of academic principles. That this policy ever existed and that it has its defenders (champions of expedience) are good reasons to remain skeptical about prospects for restoring traditional values in the schools.

Similarly, the social promotion debate illustrates the inescapable complexities of educational issues. Once the policy is altered to reinstitute merit as the basis for promotion, what is to be done with the incompetent students who formerly were merely passed along?

These students, particularly the ones who genuinely try to improve, cannot simply be discarded; the school system is obligated to make every effort to educate them. Tutoring, special classes, and summer school programs must be developed and funded, which means additional difficult searches for money and qualified personnel.

Undermining even the best intentions is the growing shortage of qualified teachers. This is caused by low salaries, diminished respect for teaching as a profession, inadequate teacher training programs, and the expanded job opportunities for women. (For most women, teaching used to be the best of the limited career options available.)

Any effort to improve the quality of the classroom "product" has several purposes. In addition to simply raising the level of academic achievement, a secondary purpose is to rally public support for the schools. Without a constituency of believers in the DISD's mission, the student population will continue to dwindle and the support needed to secure funding will wither.

Parents constitute the most important part of this public support base. In Dallas, parents have proved exceptionally willing to fight to maintain acceptable public schools. A city-wide organization, Positive Parents, advertises support for the DISD, and their volunteers man telephone lines to answer questions from parents who are considering enrolling (or re-enrolling) their children in public school. In some individual schools, parents have formed support groups that honor outstanding students, faculty, and administrators and generally boost the school's reputation in the community.

The Dallas business community also has helped to make up for the shortfall in funds. Through an "Adopt a School" program, businesses can help meet specific needs; for example, by purchasing computers for student use in a particular school.

This kind of support is growing. Corporate aid and bond election votes evidence a deep, residual faith in the schools. Parent and general community support, although having no direct policy-making role, is important because it is the base for the political organizing necessary to pass bond propositions and to elect responsible persons to the school board.

One of the most difficult problems for the DISD has been meeting the challenge of educating non-English-speaking children. This task is not unique to Dallas; in some cities the public schools are populated by speakers of more than 100 languages. In Dallas, the issue centers on Spanish-speaking children. What are the school system's responsibilities to these students? What are the best ways to teach these children?

Finding answers to such questions is a politically volatile business. This is a matter of directing scarce funds to a minority community, something that always runs the risk of alienating the Anglo population. And even among Mexican-American parents, by no means is there unanimity about the best way to educate their children.

Between 1970 and 1980, Hispanic enrollment in the DISD increased from 8.4 percent to 19.4 percent. Many of these students speak little or no English and do not hear English in their homes. When tossed into schools in which they are expected to perform in English, many of these students fare predictably badly.

Based on test results (and on common sense), it was clear that Spanish-speaking students were not actually being educated in the Dallas schools; they were merely being kept there during the school day. Litigation inevitably followed. Federal courts ordered that these students be taught — a noble idea but not easily implemented. The plan arrived at by judges and educators was bilingual education.

The theory of bilingual education is to teach young Spanish-speaking students basic skills in Spanish, gradually leading them into English, so by the end of sixth grade the students can be assimilated into regular, English-speaking classrooms. According to this theory, the student learning to read, for example, is taught first to read in Spanish so he can receive some reinforcement at home even if no family members speak English.

For anyone familiar only with traditional teaching, the bilingual classroom seems a different world. In some classes, only Spanish is spoken. In others, Spanish is spoken at some times and English at others to accommodate the non-Spanish-speaking students who, due to the teacher shortage, also must be enrolled in the schools used in the bilingual program.

The mixture of Spanish and English sounds strange, but probably this linguistic melange works to the advantage of the young students; they are likely to instinctively pick up some English even while learning their basics in Spanish.

Bilingual education is expensive and difficult to administer. The cost is a hot political issue since the parents of some of the children in the program are illegal aliens.

Within the Hispanic community, critics say bilingual education is inherently racist, designed to prevent assimilation of Hispanic youngsters into mainstream American culture. Some opponents of the program charge that "it ensures yet another generation of car wash attendants and domestics" in the Mexican-American community.

But proponents of bilingual teaching say test scores support the wisdom of this approach. The student who would be left behind in an all-English environment now is able to keep pace until he learns enough English to make that his classroom language.

One of the biggest problems facing the bilingual program is the shortage of qualified teachers. Some bilingual classrooms in Dallas must be staffed by teachers whose Spanish is fluent but who do not speak English well. This destroys the *bi*-lingual aspect of the schooling.

School district administrators and the elected DISD board have remained committed to the program because of court orders and because no one has yet come up with a better way to handle Dallas's ever-growing number of Spanish-speaking students.

The principal issue here is not merely educational method, but rather the search for a way to ensure integration of the Hispanic population into the life of the city. This does not mean that ethnic identities should be forsaken; the only result of this would be cultural sterility. The schools must do everything possible to help their graduates enter the "real world" on equal footing.

This aspect of bilingual education is too seldom considered. The current system's critics want forced immersion — instruction exclusively in English. This, however, is likely to result in many Hispanic students failing courses and graduating (if at all) near the bottom of their classes. Is this too great a price to pay for becoming more quickly conversant in the community's dominant language?

Education planners need to worry more about such matters, but long-term issues too often are neglected in the face of pressure on relatively minor points (such as personnel assignments). Too much time and effort are spent on matters that won't even be remembered a year from now.

The role of the public school system in the overall life of the community is an important issue, requiring a well-reasoned philosophy as a basis for policy formulation. This philosophy must be developed through a coherent process that enlists the participation of educators, parents, and all the other constituent groups that have a stake in the quality of education.

Persons who think of Texas as an exotic nation-state often mistakenly assume Dallas is a "wild west" town (it never really was) that offers only a raw, anti-intellectual environment, a home of modern cowboys who have exchanged their chaps and spurs for three-piece suits without bothering to become more sophisticated.

Dallas's great strides in improving its arts offerings do much to debunk this notion. Dallas also has developed a diversified system of higher education that should thoroughly dispel the myth of intellectual emptiness in the community.

The Dallas County Community College District (DCCCD), with seven campuses in and around the city, offers two-year programs with open admissions for high school graduates. Tuition is nominal for Dallas County residents. More than 50,000 students were enrolled in 1982.

The DCCCD evolved in part because of recognition that the job market demanded some middle ground between a high school diploma and a college degree. The average level of educational attainment continues to rise, with an associate degree from a two-year college often replacing the high school diploma as the minimum acceptable qualification demanded by employers.

Like the Dallas Independent School District, the Dallas County Community College District is a taxing authority with an elected board. For the most part, it has remained free from serious controversy and has maintained a high degree of public support. This is due in part to its student body's broad base, including members of all economic and racial groups. With this base, the DCCCD is politically potent and has attracted substantial financial support from foundations and individual donors, as well as deriving its principal funding from tax revenues.

This political and financial support also stems from the acceptance accorded the notion of having a community college system. Not too many years ago, such a program would have been criticized as being an unnecessary luxury provided to high school graduates. Today, the community college network is accepted as a logical part of public education offerings.

The notion of expanding the availability of higher education is as much a reflection of economic realism as it is of simple generosity. If a community's work force is to compete with other areas (both American and foreign), workers must possess fundamental skills, particularly those required by the new manufacturing and service technologies.

The egalitarian approach of the junior college system meets this particular need. These schools might not turn out a large number of eventual doctoral candidates, but they do ensure existence of an acceptable basic level of literacy and technical competence in the community. This adds a certain stability to Dallas's economic base.

The rich University of Texas system has schools in the Dallas area, and private colleges such as Southern

Methodist University attract students from around the country. But Dallas is not truly a "university town." SMU, in particular, constantly tries to define its responsibilities within the larger community.

Dallas is moving very slowly toward enhanced appreciation of what its institutions of higher education can offer. Spurred by the high tech development attracted by Austin and San Antonio, Dallas is trying to play catch-up.

The roles universities should be playing in the continuing growth of the city and region are still inadequately defined. A logical nexus could exist between private corporations and universities able to conduct extensive research and development projects. Only ad hoc measures govern such matters now. Also missing is a plan to expand the involvement of university personnel and facilities in the cultural life of Dallas.

This elusiveness of academic "community" is attributable, at least in part, to Dallas's youthfulness as a city. Local traditions are still being shaped. Intellectual life develops in spurts and stops; it cannot be planned too precisely without stripping it of vitality. And yet, there still must be a sense of purpose to motivate development of this life.

Why is the fostering of imagination so important? Why is the life of the city tied to the life of the mind? Such questions cannot be answered quickly. They require time, a rare commodity in Dallas's rush to prosperity.

While this slow process takes place, interest in Dallas's intellectual life has been stimulated by several small organizations that try to raise the level of discourse about subjects as diverse as classical literature and transit planning.

Principal among these is the Dallas Institute of Humanities and Culture, a privately-funded organization that assiduously resists being labeled a "think tank." Founded in 1980, the Institute encourages people to recognize the importance of having a philosophy on which to base action. This advocacy is a counterpoint to the high speed glibness that pervades conversation in Dallas and the high pressure avarice that characterizes much of the city's business dealings.

Slowing the city's pace to allow thinking increases chances of a person being properly sensitive to Dallas's wants and needs. In many of its programs, the Institute urges the city's leadership not to be content to merely hop-skip from crisis to crisis, but rather to give imagination a chance in the governing process.

The Institute wisely does not pretend to offer an intellectual panacea for Dallas's problems. According to Institute director Gail Thomas, its goal is "to bring thoughtful reflection to the city; for philosophical ideas to have a place alongside the practical; to have a way for imagination to meet action."

This is a goal that can well serve all the intellectual and educational life of the community. Until the goal is realized, the learning process never will achieve the rate of ascent Dallas needs.

Central Expressway *Daniel Barsotti*

V

DELIVERING HEALTH CARE

Most Americans endorse the principle of providing health care to persons who are ill and poor. Few persons quarrel with this as an abstract ideal, but when it comes to paying taxes to cover huge medical bills, idealism sometimes gives way to hard-nosed pragmatism.

Delivery of health care requires a complex system that is only partly the realm of traditional medicine. Assessment of community health needs, winning voter support for bond elections, and even transit planning to ensure that patients can reach the hospital now are among the chief concerns of hospital administrators.

Of the more than 8,000 hospital beds in Dallas, most are in private hospitals, but nearly 1,000 are at Parkland Memorial Hospital, the public facility that serves the indigent population of Dallas County.

On Parkland falls the burden of representing the community's collective conscience as provider of medical care. This hospital's operations offer lessons in urban governance as well as in health care delivery.

Parkland is something of an anomaly in American public medicine. While other public hospitals have struggled (some unsuccessfully) to keep their doors open when revenues declined and patient loads increased, Parkland not only eliminated its operating deficit, but it has done so without compromising the quality of care it offers its mostly poor patients.

Rigorous cost containment procedures at the hospital and strong public support for needed taxes and bonds have buoyed Parkland's fortunes. By fiscal 1981, Parkland had a surplus of over $6 million.

A public hospital's finances, however, are inextricably tied to national and local economic conditions. As the recession of the early 1980s took hold, Parkland found its number of non-paying patients climbing at an alarming rate. When a worker loses his job, he usually also loses his health insurance. Many private hospitals turn away uninsured patients. These people then end up at hospitals such as Parkland that are legally obligated to accept anyone needing care.

This recession-generated influx of patients was enough to drive Parkland's budget into the red. By fiscal 1982, the surplus had turned into a deficit of almost $1.7 million.

Parkland's financial state is the subject of often heated political debate. A hospital board appointed by the Dallas County Commissioners governs the hospital and recommends a budget.

The commissioners approve or alter that budget and set the appropriate tax rate to fund it. Even politicians who have praised Parkland become surly at the prospect of having to raise taxes.

The dollar figures in these matters are substantial. In fiscal 1982, Parkland's revenues totaled $110.9 million, $63.1 million (58%) coming from hospital district taxes.

The magnitude of Parkland's patient flow is comparable to that of the flow of funds. Annual admissions total more than 43,000, eighty percent of which come via the emergency room. The outpatient clinics see approximately 225,000 visits per year.

Parkland's constituency is large. Hospital administrators spend considerable time trying to determine the medical needs of Dallas's indigents.

Debate continues about the role of satellite clinics in high-need parts of the community. One problem with dispersing medical treatment centers is the cost of much of the hardware involved; it simply isn't practical to duplicate many of the services available at the hospital.

Another issue is that of management of neighborhood clinics. Some community organizations want to run the clinics in their neighborhoods, but this can prove disastrous. One Dallas clinic that became a focal point for local political bickering has faced being closed by the Department of Health and Human Services because of gross mismanagement.

The choice, in simplest terms, is between delivering health services to neighborhoods and delivering the people who need the services to the hospital.

This choice must be made carefully in light of the experiences of other hospitals, such as Philadelphia General. In Philadelphia, decentralization of care via community clinics became the governing theory for public medicine. The central hospital's operations were scaled down in anticipation of opening new clinics throughout the parts of the city most needing public health care. But the clinics never developed as planned, the main hospital (Philadelphia General) closed, and the city's poor found themselves hard-pressed to locate adequate medical care.

Recognizing the difficulty of striking the appropriate balance between centralized and neighborhood health care, some in Dallas have suggested that transit planning become a part of the overall health care scheme. As Dallas develops its long-range mass transit plan, movement of people to Parkland could be one of the criteria for routing light rail or expanded bus service.

Such a transit route is expensive, but it is responsive to the need for better access to Parkland. It also is more sensible, both economically and logistically, than relying too heavily on a network of neighborhood clinics.

While hospital administrators grapple with the problem of how best to serve their constituency, they also must devote some attention to maintaining Parkland's ties to the rest of Dallas's medical community. In some cities, the public hospital becomes the medical profession's stepchild, shunned by doctors, potential fund donors, and most of the community as being merely a dispenser of "poor people's medicine."

Parkland's doctors admit the volume of patients necessitates limits on how personalized care can be, but they say the quality of care they provide is excellent. One reason for such excellence is the hospital's relationship with the University of Texas's Southwestern Medical School.

Parkland is a teaching hospital, providing the clinical setting essential to a doctor's training. In turn, the Southwestern faculty without charge provides supervision of care for Parkland patients. Southwestern, with its strong reputation among medical schools, attracts top students and faculty, thus ensuring high quality staffing at Parkland. This marriage between the two institutions works well.

The medical community's willingness to work at Parkland (in addition to or instead of affiliating with the more lavish private hospitals) depends largely on doctors' confidence in Parkland's facilities and administration, which, in turn, are dependent on political support from the commissioners and from the public.

Sometimes local politicians find it difficult to distinguish Parkland from other recipients of tax dollars. Parkland, of course, *is* different; it is in the business of saving lives. Although the politicians love to tinker with the hospital district's tax rate and enjoy quibbling over picayune items in Parkland's budget, the public is more openhearted.

In 1980, in a hospital district bond election to approve $80 million in bond financing for expansion, the hospital received a 71 percent favorable vote, with support coming evenly from throughout the community.

Survey research conducted during this campaign found high public regard for Parkland, particularly for its emergency room. When asked which Dallas-area hospital is best equipped to handle emergencies, 86 percent of poll respondents favored Parkland. The same survey found public support of the general notion of local government providing health care for persons who cannot afford to pay for it; the margin was 81-12, in favor.

The survey research offered proof that Parkland has avoided the stigma that plagues many public hospitals: the belief that the charity hospital is merely a place for deadbeats, providing no benefits to the community at large. Parkland is seen as a "poor people's hospital," but it is accepted as an essential, general services hospital as well.

Political consciousness among Parkland's staff members is necessitated by perpetual fears of funding shortfalls. This is the continuing problem in providing health care in American cities. With populations in the hundreds of thousands, many of whom are either poor or at least incapable of paying the astronomic costs of hospitalization, what alternative do cities have to using unlimited amounts of public money to take care of these people?

In other cities, rationing care has been tried. This policy is as simple as it is controversial: Only so much free or low-cost care is made available; when that quota is reached, the care stops.

For example, assume a hospital has 500 beds, 50 of which are reserved for charity (non-paying) patients. Of these beds, 300 are filled, including all 50 of the charity beds. Someone comes to the hospital, needing care but unable to pay. Since the ration of free care for the moment has been exhausted, the prospective patient is turned away. Where does he go?

This sounds heartless and, according to some doctors, is unethical. But some hospital administrators say that this practice is the only way they can survive, that hospital care is *not* a "right" and therefore has its limits.

Parkland has rejected rationing. Its chief executive officer, Dr. Ron Anderson, has said he would resign rather than refuse care to someone who needs it.

So far, the issue has not attracted much public attention in Dallas. As the 1980 survey research indicates, there is little resentment about publicly funded medical care for indigents. Based on the landslide win in the 1980 hospital bond election, voters are likely to support reasonable increases in hospital district taxes if necessary to maintain Parkland's open door policy.

Public faith in Parkland results not only from sound management and reliable medical care, but also from the public relations effort the hospital undertakes to keep its constituency informed of its successes. Self-serving hyperbole is remarkably absent; the hospital has a good reputation among local news media for being straightforward and reliable.

The image-building is extremely important to the hospital, because if public support wanes, Parkland would become an appealing target for politicians on budget-slashing forays. Without broad-based political strength, Parkland might be unable to handle the crushing financial difficulties that have overwhelmed so many other public hospitals.

While Parkland does well in performing the traditional duties of a public hospital, Dallas, like most other cities, suffers from inadequate responsiveness to mental health needs.

Responsibility for mental health services is widely dispersed among numerous public and private agencies. The local Mental Health and Mental Retardation Center (MHMR) is the county agency responsible for treatment and for the administrative complexities of evaluating patients and sending them to appropriate state facilities.

MHMR, however, is short on funds and long on bureaucracy. The MHMR caseload is perpetually at capacity. A person seeking help from the agency will be referred elsewhere unless he has a history of psychiatric hospitalization or appears severely dysfunctional. This person then must sift through a variety of private agencies to find care. The Mental Health Association, a private agency funded primarily by the United Way, tries to serve as a clearinghouse. It refers persons to other appropriate agencies and sponsors programs such as foster parent education and child abuse prevention training.

Size and effectiveness are not necessarily compatible. The diversity of Dallas's mental health agency offerings is impressive, but the person needing these services often finds himself uncertain where to turn. He can call a "hot line" telephone service that might or might not be able to respond appropriately. For the person needing help, the prospect of having to sort through offerings of various agencies is likely to be daunting to the point of making the effort seem useless.

Enlightenment on mental health issues has been slow in coming. Even as it arrives, it has not been accompanied by the same diligence in providing delivery of services that more traditional medical matters have received.

Money is part of this problem. No funding exists to develop a comprehensive mental health services system. Parkland Hospital's psychiatric emergency room and other treatment facilities do their jobs well when patients finally reach them, but these facilities tend to operate in vacuums, knowing little about what related agencies are doing. Preventive medicine, a particularly important part of mental health care, cannot survive without coherent, system-wide planning.

The most logical resolution of these problems is first to better coordinate existing services and then to make mental health treatment more readily accessible to people needing it. Expanded MHMR funding would allow a more realistic availability of mental health professionals, thus making Dallas one of the first communities to treat mental health care as a legitimate and significant social service.

The prognosis for health care in Dallas is optimistic. The resources are there: a good hospital and medical school, widespread support for public health services, skilled professionals working with dedicated volunteers, and genuine concern about people in need receiving the services they require.

Increased sophistication in coordinating these services remains necessary. That certainly is within Dallas's reach if more people decide to make health care a top priority for the community.

Surls' sculpture installation, One Dallas Centre *Daniel Barsotti*

VI

THE CASE FOR THE ARTS

If "the business of Dallas is business," is there room in the city's life for the arts? For many years, the answer to that question was merely "perhaps."

Wholehearted, broad-based support for the arts in Dallas was late in coming. Not surprisingly, it wasn't until strong economic arguments could be made in favor of the arts that cultural institutions moved into the mainstream of the city's life.

In Texas, an art genre exists known as "the bluebonnet school." Painters have turned out thousands of landscape canvasses covered with the Texas state flower. All these paintings look remarkably alike — the hazy blue field of flowers, perhaps with an oil rig in the background just in case anyone might forget where this scene is located.

More serious art also has found a home in Texas and particularly in Dallas. The 1930s saw the heyday of Texas's "regionalist" artists, led by Dallas painters including Jerry Bywaters, Otis Dozier, and Alexander Hogue. The regionalists' colorful realism won praise from critics, but most of Dallas did not seem to view the arts as an important aspect of the community's life.

Even when Dallas opened a new art museum on the State Fairgrounds as part of the 1936 state centennial, there was little noticeable broadening of taste or of long-term support for the arts. (Only after a half century of relative neglect did the regionalist artists receive a new round of overdue praise when the Dallas Museum of Art mounted its 1985 exhibition, "Lone Star Regionalism.")

As Dallas grew during the next several decades, opportunities to make money abounded; culture could wait. Some people began using their wealth to build superb private art collections and to travel to places where the arts flourished, but the public's cultural opportunities remained limited.

Slowly, this began to change. For example, in 1957 the Dallas Civic Opera was born, with Maria Callas as the featured artist in several early productions. Only a half-filled auditorium greeted Callas for her first appearance in November, 1957, but her performance drew such national acclaim that Dallas society soon realized the city had a treasure at hand. After hearing Callas, one business leader told the Opera's director, "This is even better than 'My Fair Lady.'" That man promptly became chairman of the opera's board. From such beginnings, the corps of arts patrons began to grow.

By the early 1970s, a new sophistication was beginning to appear on the Dallas arts scene. The Museum of Fine Arts hired as its director Harry Parker, who had been assistant director of the Metropolitan Museum in New York. Parker's charge was to move the Dallas museum once and for all away from any lingering influence of "the bluebonnet school," rally the loyalties (and funds) of likely arts patrons, and develop a world-class museum.

While Parker gradually expanded the museum's collection, the Dallas Symphony Orchestra hired one of the world's most promising conductors, Eduardo Mata of Mexico, as music director. The opera continued to flourish. The popularity of the Dallas Ballet surged. The Dallas Theater Center offered a repertoire mixing traditional and avant garde productions. New arts organizations began to sprout. Attendance at arts events undoubtedly was helped by the influx of new Dallasites who had immigrated from cities where the arts had been well established.

In hard numbers, however, this cadre of supporters remained but a small part of the Dallas population. In any community, the true test of arts organizations is their ability to develop a constituency that is representative of the entire local citizenry.

By 1978, arts leaders and Dallas city officials were confident enough about the popular appeal of the arts to submit a $45 million arts bond proposition to the voters. The money would be used for a new art museum, a concert hall, and other cultural facilities and programs. On the advice of a confident mayor and other local politicians, arts organizations did little campaigning. The bond proposition lost by a margin of 54-46 percent.

The principal flaw in the campaign plan was the assumption that the general public was sold on the idea of the arts as an essential aspect of a city's life. Instead, most voters looked on the arts as extravagant frills. One radio commentator referred to the proposed new art museum as "a pleasure palace for the rich." The election results and post-campaign voter surveys proved that voters believed such accusations of elitism.

The art museum immediately began planning another try for bond money in 1979. Aside from meeting the requirements of a full-fledged campaign, the museum found itself redefining its position in the community. Who were its friends? What did the average Dallas resident think of the arts? How detrimental and correctable was the "elitist" image that hung as a political albatross on the arts organizations?

Survey research commissioned by the museum found discouraging answers. Relatively few Dallasites said they had much interest or stake in the arts. Dallas arts institutions (particularly the museum and the symphony, the organizations that would be testing the voters again in 1979) recognized they would have to appeal not just to the most devoted arts aficionados, but rather to the city as a whole.

Special efforts also would have to be made to convince city council members that the arts institutions were politically viable. No politician wants to back a loser, and, based on the 1978 bond election results, arts organizations were losers.

Popularizing the arts occurred in various ways. Most of the arts organizations expanded their "outreach" programs to increase community participation in the arts. Schoolchildren, senior citizens, minorities, and other identifiable population groups were targeted for special concerts, museum tours, and the like. These efforts let more people see the diversity and accessibility of arts offerings. This, the arts leaders hoped, would help erase their elitist image.

One of the most important elements in expanding the arts constituency was the exhibition in Dallas in early 1979 of "Pompeii AD 79," a blockbuster show that attracted over 370,000 visitors to the art museum during its 13-week run. Many of these people never had been in the museum before. The museum collected names of thousands of the visitors and later solicited these people for funds and votes.

Underlying such efforts was the growing realization that arts organizations are, to a considerable extent, political entities. Unless they are members of that rare breed operating with no need for public support, cultural institutions must observe some of the niceties of political decorum.

These public relations endeavors, coupled with a well-funded and politically sophisticated campaign, led to bond election victories for the museum and symphony in November 1979. The museum won approval of $24.9 million in bond funding for land and construction of its new facility; the symphony won authorization for $2.3 million towards purchase of land for its new concert hall.

In 1982, the symphony ran another bond campaign,

this time for $28.6 million to be used to build the hall. Once again, the symphony followed the rules of good politics, reaching out to identifiable voter blocs and running a professionally managed campaign with a budget of approximately $300,000. And, once again, the symphony was successful, winning 57 percent of the vote.

By the conclusion of the 1982 campaign, all the arts organizations in Dallas — those that had been in campaigns already and those such as the Dallas Opera that were contemplating future bond elections — recognized the inescapable ties between the arts and politics. Retreating into the comfortable cocoon of elitism no longer was possible.

Politicians at city hall were taking note of the new political consciousness of arts organizations. Initial fears that inept "artsy-craftsy" campaigning would hurt other items on the bond ballot gave way to admiration for the political professionalism with which the arts campaigns were run.

This city hall approval is crucial in Dallas because of the high degree of governmental involvement in the arts. The Dallas Museum of Arts, for example, has its own board of trustees that hires its director and is responsible for museum policy-making. The museum building, however, is owned by the city, as is most of the art. The city provides approximately $1.2 million annually for museum operations.

Construction of the new museum was a joint venture, with the city providing the funds (through issuance of general obligation bonds) for 75 percent of land purchase and 60 percent of construction. The museum raised the remainder from private donors.

This partnership usually works well. Rarely do elected officials or city administrators try to meddle with arts organizations' operations. Some political tension is maintained, however, since the arts institutions must submit budget requests annually to the city council. This in turn makes it necessary for directors of these institutions to develop enough lobbying expertise to ensure that council members are kept informed about and pleased with arts activities. As with the political imperatives of bond campaigns, this city hall maneuvering underscores the permanence of the marriage between the arts and politics.

The city government treads a narrow path between providing support for the arts and becoming actively involved in arts programming itself. The City Arts Program, a part of the Parks and Recreation Department, has served mainly as a coordinator of facilities and an expediter of administrative necessities. Dallas so far has resisted the temptation to create a full-fledged Arts and Culture Department that would produce its own programs. Whenever this idea has surfaced, so has opposition to the notion of government becoming an actual participant in arts decision-making.

With a cooperative city government and consistently generous private assistance from individuals and businesses, Dallas arts organizations never have become overly reliant on federal largesse. As a result, Dallas has been spared the fiscal trauma suffered by so many cities when the Reagan administration slashed federal aid to arts programs.

Although the major Dallas arts institutions are in good financial shape, smaller arts organizations have trouble maintaining fiscal equilibrium. A top-heavy pattern of financial support causes problems if donors become so accustomed to giving to monuments that they forget the importance of individual as well as institutional initiative in the arts.

New arts projects spring up regularly in Dallas. Some innovative theaters, for example, have kept exceptional young talents — many of them native to Dallas — in Dallas instead of following the traditional paths to New York, Los Angeles, and elsewhere.

Efforts of Dallas's young arts entrepreneurs, however, too often go unnoticed in the rush to hop aboard the glamorous bandwagons of larger arts organizations. As a result, many of these nascent projects quickly fall into precarious financial condition, and the young talent of the city is forced to reconsider the decision to remain in Dallas.

Some of the more aggressive theater producers and gallery directors have realized that they will find only limited success among the "old guard" donors whose loyalties have been so carefully nurtured by the established arts institutions. So the newer organizations are trying to build a new generation of board members and donors. If they can do this, they will have taken an important step towards ensuring continuing vitality for the arts in Dallas.

The end-product of the electoral successes of the arts organizations is a remarkably ambitious project: the Dallas Arts District.

Located in the heart of downtown, the district

covers 60 acres acquired by private and city purchase (some of the latter via eminent domain). Rather than an "arts park" devoted exclusively to arts facilities, this will be a mixture of institutions such as the new museum and concert hall, several churches and historic buildings, and new, privately-owned office buildings.

With land in this part of downtown selling for more than $200 per square foot, some critics have charged that it is ridiculous to deprive the city tax rolls of revenue-producing commercial properties in favor of tax-exempt arts buildings. But in a downtown that is remarkably sterile — with streets that are windy canyons between office towers, seldom traveled even by day, and totally deserted at night — the arts district was envisioned as a way to bring some life to downtown. This kind of project, city officials and arts patrons said, would enhance daily life for businesses located there, thus providing an incentive to remain in downtown rather than fleeing to the suburbs. This kind of commercial flight has wrecked tax bases of other cities.

The district also would be an attraction for tourists, who have had little to draw them (and the money they spend) to downtown Dallas except to the maudlin but well-visited Kennedy assassination site.

Perhaps most important, the arts district was envisioned as something that would give Dallas residents a stake in their own downtown. Even persons who work downtown rarely wander far from their job locations. Virtually no one goes downtown after dark or on weekends. Retail stores have moved steadily away from downtown to uptown or suburban shopping centers. Even though Dallas's center is far less frightening to drivers than are most cities, few Dallas residents consider going downtown unless absolutely necessary.

Many government and business leaders liked the arts district concept. They saw it as a mark of distinction for Dallas and a means to further enhance the value of downtown real estate. Located on the north edge of the central business district, the arts zone could prove a perfect bridge to the relatively undeveloped properties that likely would be parts of a much-expanded downtown of the future.

The economic argument for the arts district's benefits for downtown is reflective of the fiscal issues that mix constantly with arts matters in Dallas. Crucial to the art museum bond proposition in 1979 was an economic impact study conducted during the Pompeii exhibition that proved the arts not only were not a financial burden on a city, but even could contribute significantly to a city's fiscal health.

The Pompeii study demonstrated how out-of-town visitors who came to Dallas principally to see Pompeii pumped over $8 million into the city in 13 weeks. Hotels, restaurants, retail stores, other arts institutions, and many other elements of the Dallas economy directly benefited from this spending. Even the tax-free status of the museum property became a supportive argument: Although no property tax revenues would be generated directly by the museum property, the presence of the museum would enhance neighboring property values, thus increasing their assessed worth and, in turn, their tax payments.

Such arguments were crucial because the museum's survey research showed that even persons supporting the general idea of a new art museum began backing away in the face of the building's $40 million price tag and the fear that the museum would prove a drain on city resources. Even arts supporters don't like tax increases.

When the symphony launched its 1982 campaign, one of its first political salvos was release of its own economic impact study including many of the arguments the museum had advanced earlier. The study also stressed the additional jobs construction of the concert hall would provide. This argument worked well with voters worried about the recession that was so pervasive at the time of the symphony's bond vote.

The importance assigned to these economic issues illustrates the pragmatic nature of Dallas's approach to the arts. Purely aesthetic concerns produce only limited responses from government and business leaders whose principal interest is "the bottom line." To their credit, Dallas arts organizations recognize this and incorporate sophisticated economic projections in virtually all their planning.

The result is an increasingly strong relationship not only between the arts and city government, but also between arts organizations and private business. This in turn results in an enviable independence for arts entities that are tied by law to city hall but need more than city assistance if they are truly to prosper. Businessmen respect good business sense; they have found this to an initially unexpected degree in the major arts institutions.

In addition to these economic factors, the arts district is likely to ameliorate the stark, overwhelming physical presence of downtown Dallas.

As in most major cities, Dallas's downtown is "vertical," with skyscrapers of ever-increasing height being packed ever more densely within the central business district. Downtown becomes inhospitable to pedestrians and to anyone who wants to wander rather than to plunge headlong from one office building to the next.

The arts district will offer some respite from the vertical city syndrome. The museum, the district's west anchor, is long and low. Moving east from it is a grand boulevard along which set-back restrictions on new construction should enhance the feeling of breadth. Farther to the east (about four blocks from the museum) will stand the concert hall. Within the district already are a historic mansion that serves as the local bar association headquarters, Roman Catholic and Methodist churches, and the Arts Magnet High School.

All these buildings are under four stories high. Mixed amongst these structures will be a number of high-rise office towers, but their designs will be compatible with the overall design of the district and will feature stair-step facades so the pedestrian within the arts district will not be struck by the immediacy of overwhelming building height.

The mix of low and high buildings is rare, but it is preferable — because it is more realistic land use — to an "arts campus" approach that would make the arts district more of a park, with no mixed-use aspects.

Early arts district advocates envisioned just this kind of park approach as the way to create the district. But city planners, joined by some influential arts patrons, argued that the park concept would be pretty but sterile. The key to making an arts district work is to have people there; under-visited arts facilities are a waste, however they are designed and wherever they are located. With commercial as well as arts development in the district, a consistently large, flowing population is assured.

People who work in the office towers probably will be among the most frequent visitors to the museum and to lunchtime concerts in the new symphony hall. They will be principal patrons of the district's retail stores, which are expected to include a number of commercial galleries, bookstores, and other businesses that will appeal to arts-oriented shoppers.

The goal of arts district planners is to shape an area that is both busy and relaxed — a home for active street life and healthy retail activity as well as for the relative quiet that will allow people to enjoy art and find respite from the city's commercial rush.

A more elusive goal is to introduce residential development in or near the arts district. Every large city wants people to live downtown to prevent the deadening impact of the weekday 5 PM exodus and the arid emptiness of weekends. Activity within the arts district should help with such matters but cannot wholly compensate for the lack of a permanent population base.

Within the past several years, new upper-middle income housing (townhouses and condominium apartments) has been built on the outskirts of the central business district. The largest of these relatively small, experimental projects have proved successful. Development of more residential areas within downtown has been barred by prohibitively high land costs. Texas legislation does, however, allow some tax incentives and funding assistance for central city areas. Although these programs are designed primarily for depressed urban areas (which the Dallas arts district certainly isn't), downtown residential growth might be deemed important enough to generate new legislation that would allow some kind of incentives.

For this substantial part of downtown, Dallas has tied its future to the arts. That this linkage between economic and aesthetic development exists is appropriately "Dallas-like."

So far, the arts-politics-business troika seems to be working well. The alliance is always going to be tenuous; competing, as well as shared, interests abound. But almost all of the community now recognizes that a city needs an active cultural life. The voters now have repeatedly said they want outstanding arts facilities; city hall and business leaders agree.

As the arts (in the collective sense) continue to become more sophisticated and more organizationally complex, some new coordinating efforts likely will be necessary. The idea of creating an "arts council" in Dallas has frightened the larger arts organizations. They fear that implicit in such a "council" would be a commitment to joint fund raising that could divert funds from the most successful institutions and channel them to the more needy organizations. This outlook might be greedy, but with donors' dollars increasingly hard to find, greed has become a necessary part of survival.

Some coordination, however, among arts organizations is essential. The intricate maneuverings of city hall politics demand continuous monitoring and adroit responsiveness. Despite the competition for funding, there remains a basic common cause for the arts — to ensure that government not return to the philosophy that arts are frills to be taken care of only if there is extra money in the budget.

Arts lobbying in Dallas rarely has achieved the sophistication that it has on the federal level, where the White House, executive agencies, and Congress direct a variety of funding and programming efforts. But since the city holds title to most major Dallas arts facilities, assuming continued governmental benevolence is inherently risky; too much is at stake.

Dallas arts patrons have paid only sporadic attention to city council campaigns. With the expansions of the city's arts establishment and city hall's role in arts governance, leaders of arts organizations probably will selectively contribute to more council candidates. A coordinating body might be established to quietly monitor this political activity. In other words, arts organizations are starting to behave like any other special interest group.

The arts district poses some additional challenges to arts governance. The administration of the district has been entrusted not to City Hall but to citizen boards composed of arts leaders, the district's private landowners, and representatives of various city constituencies. How much power should this extra-governmental entity wield? How long will the city council keep its hands off arts district management?

By early 1985, the district's self-government apparatus was in place and working well. But a peaceful, cooperative relationship between city government and the arts will require constant nurturing.

None of these matters can be resolved easily. The development of the arts is accompanied by growing pains, some of which evolve from matters that traditionally have been far removed from the aesthetic considerations on which arts organizations and their patrons would prefer to concentrate.

But these people have enjoyed the rapid transformation of Dallas's cultural life from small-town level to nearly world-class excellence, and it is likely that they now will do whatever is necessary — including dabbling in politics — to ensure the continued health of the arts in Dallas.

Pocket park, Downtown Dallas *Daniel Barsotti*

VII

THE OTHER DALLAS: POVERTY IN THE MIDST OF PLENTY

Despite its image as a wealthy city, Dallas by no means has escaped the poverty that plagues urban America.

Problems of the poor have not become as severe here as they are in many other cities. The unemployment rate, for example, never has reached the excruciating heights cities such as Detroit have known. Only a small percentage of Dallas residents receive welfare. In Dallas County, 30,000 persons receive Aid for Families with Dependent Children (AFDC), and 20,000 of these citizens are children. The average monthly AFDC payment is $53 per month and 70% of the persons who go on AFDC stay on for less than a year.

But a certain dissonance emanates from the poor of Dallas and disrupts the self-congratulatory chorus of praise for Dallas life.

Dallas's wealth is evident in countless ways: the shiny architecture of public and private buildings, the sleek cars crowding expressways, the opulent stores, posh restaurants, and new businesses that become bonanzas overnight.

All these highly visible facets of Dallas life shape the city's image. The world has accepted the notion of Dallas providing a rich and vibrant lifestyle for its citizens.

There is, however, another Dallas — a city rarely seen by outsiders and too seldom noticed by most Dallas citizens. This other Dallas is rarely touched by the rays of wealth that brighten most of the city. It is populated largely by blacks, Hispanics, Asians, and Native Americans, groups that together constitute more than half of Dallas's population. It is plagued disproportionately by crime, inadequate city service, joblessness, and the other most severe ills of modern urban America.

City Hall officials periodically take notice of the problems of the poor. When the abundant resources of this city are directed toward solving a problem, they usually can accomplish much. But a preliminary difficulty is that of getting most citizens simply to recognize that these issues exist.

A large part of this problem in Dallas (as in most cities) stems from relative levels of political participation. The poorest parts of the city — those that most need friends in elective office — consistently fail to vote in numbers even vaguely comparable to the balloting in the most affluent parts of town. As a result, elected officials who divide the budget pie are slow to respond to the neediest part of the city.

Since no obvious political profit is to be derived from championing the cause of the poor, and since altruism is a scarce political commodity, the other Dallas languishes while the rest of the city prospers.

Most politicians elected from the poorest parts of the city have been notably ineffective. They have seemed intent on securing their own political base by loudly echoing their constituents' demands, but after making some noise they have been content to return to their districts with empty hands, claiming to have fought the good fight against an insensitive majority.

This is the lazy way out. It keeps most constituents satisfied (if disillusioned), but it forsakes the hard work of coalition-building and developing policies that can win broad-based support in governing bodies and from the citywide electorate.

While the politicians pursue their own interests, their poorly represented constituents try to muddle through. As a class, "the poor" are not easily identified. Racial or other census-type categorizations cannot adequately encompass the wide range of persons who populate the city's lower strata.

You don't have to be a sociologist to find the poor in Dallas. In downtown, street people wander, often the sole occupants of the barren nighttime sidewalks. They sleep under scraps of metal and cardboard, relying on hand-out meals from charities.

By early 1985, this street population was estimated as at least 10,000 homeless persons. The count isn't comparable to the hordes of homeless in a city such as New York, but some of the social workers who deal with these people daily point out that the Dallas approach has been to pretend the problem doesn't even exist. The closest thing to an official city policy toward street people has been the makeshift response of the police: to jail them for vagrancy, jaywalking, or any other convenient charge.

The simplistic response to the street people is to dismiss them as bums who just happen to be passing through Dallas and who don't deserve help. In addition to the transients, however, new categories of the helpless and homeless are growing.

Mentally ill persons prematurely discharged from state institutions find themselves on the streets because local mental health programs that were supposed to help them are inadequate (or simply don't exist).

Some elderly persons — who because of accident, neglect, or abuse have failed to pay the rent or have otherwise run afoul of courts or bill collectors — are also finding themselves homeless.

"No place to go" is one of the most frightening phrases in our language. We are hearing it more often, particularly from older persons who understood life in simpler times and cannot comprehend all that whirls around them in the modern boomtown.

Dallas is in danger of being so intent on maintaining the imagery of glittering growth that these people (as well as others in the ranks of the poor, especially large numbers of women) are being left behind, discards in the rush to grow and to compound wealth as quickly as possible.

In a city of almost a million persons, overlooking the plight of these few citizens might seem understandable. But to justify the abandonment of anyone demeans the city as a whole. This fundamental moral issue has yet to be adequately addressed by Dallas's government and by the majority of its citizens.

The larger numbers of the poor are those who might, unfortunately, be considered the "traditional" poor: minority group members who cluster principally in the southern and western parts of the city.

For these people, urban life is a constant battle against despair and viciousness. Their lives are far removed from the picture statisticians can paint when showing that the Dallas crime rate has been kept relatively controlled in recent years, with many parts of town seeing marked decreases in burglaries and violent crimes.

While most of Dallas passes its nights quietly, police cars flash through some areas in dangerous (and often futile) efforts to keep the lid on. In parts of South and East Dallas, it is easy to find drug dealers conducting business on street corners and prostitutes plying their trade openly, and it isn't uncommon to hear the stacatto of pistol shots coming from the grubby apartment complexes that have become underworld arenas.

The existence of this "war zone" isn't merely ignored by most of Dallas; most persons don't have the vaguest idea that it is there. This also is the case for the monstrous health problems that plague the poor areas of Dallas.

Rates of teenage pregnancy, venereal disease, and suicide in Dallas are far higher than the national averages. The young people whose lives have been translated into these depressing statistics are mostly black and brown. This new generation is likely to be broken in health and spirit before reaching adulthood unless the city reverses its de facto policy of neglect.

This *can* be done. In West Dallas, approximately 70 percent of the population under age 19 is registered with the Dallas Children and Youth Project, which is Dallas's only comprehensive health care organization with multiple neighborhood clinics.

During its 15-year history, the Children and Youth Project has achieved remarkable results: By 1984, infant mortality among project registrants had dropped 88 percent; teenage pregnancy decreased 34 percent in nine years; and hospitalizations were reduced 62 percent over a six-year period when compared to non-registrants.

But such success is the exception, not the rule. Occasionally, conferences are held and task forces organized by well-meaning persons who can temporarily muster some indignation. These people might want to help, but they usually lack the staying power and political clout essential if policies are to be changed and worthwhile programs initiated.

Neither the city government nor the community's business establishment has said, "Something is wrong here and we're going to fix it."

Dallas is leadership-oriented; citizens expect their elected officials and business leaders to spot problems and propose solutions. If that leadership cadre doesn't act, most Dallasites assume the problems aren't significant — or aren't even there. Of course, such inaction expands the divisions between haves and have-nots in the city.

An example of this kind of sluggishness is the tardiness that has characterized the city's approach to economic development in the poorest sections of Dallas. Not until 1983 did newly-elected Mayor Starke Taylor launch a comprehensive study of South Dallas, with particular emphasis on finding ways to generate jobs and thus to elevate the standard of living in the area.

The mayor's task force found an economic wasteland in the heart of the supposedly economically invincible city. No one should have been surprised by this; the problem had been festering for years.

Initial response to the study was a far cry from the aggressive approach that has characterized Dallas's growth. Although property in South Dallas is close to the heart of downtown and is remarkably inexpensive, no one seemed eager to propose a scheme for light industry, office towers, and residential renewal.

The principal reason for such sluggish response was a simple one: No one wanted to be the first to venture into such unpromising territory.

South Dallas seemed to be considered an inoperable tumor in an otherwise healthy body, and as such should be isolated (only because it couldn't be excised), not treated.

Why this reluctance that is so contrary to Dallas's normal never-say-die philosophy? Race certainly is a major factor in discouraging prompt action.

De facto segregation is rampant in Dallas. In housing patterns, recreation, business and virtually every other aspect of Dallas life, minorities and whites rarely mix. In itself, that is not unusual; the same thing happens throughout America.

The situation is made more serious by the apparent lack of progress in building bridges between Anglo and minority communities. The formal and informal white leadership of the city is perceived by minorities as being a closed club, unwilling to share power or even to provide entry level access to the decision-making process.

For example, in Dallas's major law firms (traditional centers of political and financial clout in Dallas) black lawyers are virtually nonexistent. And although 15 percent of Dallas's citizens are Hispanic, as late as 1984 no Mexican-American had reached the upper levels of the city manager's staff.

South and West Dallas are like foreign states to many persons. Most upper-income Dallas residents don't know anything about these parts of town except that they don't want to go there. The theory seems to be, "If we ignore the problem, it might just disappear."

Of course, discrimination and economic blight don't "just disappear." They can be conquered, but not through political cowardice. The problems are complex; they can be resolved only by devising sophisticated solutions.

This means mobilizing Dallas's considerable financial expertise and economic resources. Incentives such as tax breaks and bond assistance could encourage businesses to locate in areas that now are economically stagnant.

Some locations need their own miniature master plans. For example, the art deco state fairgrounds at Fair Park (in the center of one of South Dallas's roughest areas) could be better used, both for entertainment and as a home for trade shows and other activities that require the park's ample exhibition space. These activities in turn might stimulate hotel, restaurant, and retail development in the area.

The key is persistence. Too many city councils have looked at the economically struggling parts of Dallas, decided that something should be done, commissioned studies, applauded the studies' results, and then let the status quo remain undisturbed. Dealing with the problems of affluence — such as North Dallas traffic — is more attractive than wrestling with poverty.

This approach is expedient, and given the electoral realities of the city, such neglect probably could continue for another decade.

Eventually, however, the untreated blight that afflicts impoverished parts of Dallas will spread. It will happen slowly — a few more houses will be abandoned, some dilapidated multi-family units will be condemned, several more businesses will move to the suburbs — and unless reversed this attrition will ruin the city's tax base and its image.

When urban decay passes a certain point (the exact measure is unquantifiable), Dallas will find itself facing the economic and social malaise other cities have found so crippling. By that time, it might be too late to respond.

Some of the elected officials and others who try to respond to these issues have come to realize that few of their plans — however well-intentioned and well-designed — are going to find much support in the minority community unless these ideas are aggressively sold by the Anglo leadership that for so long has appeared remote and uncaring.

To the most diligent of these persons (such as Mayor Starke Taylor, who initiated the South Dallas economic plan), it might seem unfair to have to overcome a presumption of guilt before their policies can be tested. That, however, is the inescapable result of so many years of inattentiveness.

Dallas's racial schisms are fueled by a "benign neglect" that pervades race relations in Dallas.

This is seen, for example, in what most charitably can be called naivete in the police department's belated recognition that many persons in the minority community still see police officers not as protectors of lives and property, but as insensitive, trigger-happy oppressors. Minority citizens are the hardest hit by crime, but many don't trust the police. By logical extension, they don't trust the city government that controls the police.

Another factor contributing to racial friction is the performance of the local news media. Partly because of a lack of minority journalists in Dallas, a preponderance of news covered in the minority community has to do with crime and other aspects of urban decay. Problems need to be reported, but so, too, do the achievements in business, the arts, religion, and other elements of minority life in Dallas.

News reports shortchange these matters.

The negative tone in much news coverage of the minority community is a two-edged sword. Not only does it damage minority group members' self-image, but also it perpetuates the worst stereotypes about minorities.

The litany of race-related problems seems to have no end. As long as these problems fail to be addressed aggressively, they will fester, and the divisions between the races and between economic classes will expand.

Downtown Dalpark *Daniel Barsotti*

VIII
SHAPING THE FUTURE

Dallas's prospects are bright. The city's continued prosperity seems secure. Problems do exist but appear soluble, assuming Dallas devotes appropriate resources and energy to finding solutions.

Many people in Dallas figure they should worry solely about maintaining the status quo and keeping open their options. Things are good, these people reason, and they can only get better.

That sanguine approach to the future is inherently dangerous. Dallas is still a young city, and as it moves beyond its adolescence it will face new tests. Within the next few years, Dallas either will embark on an ambitious program of carefully planned growth, or it will enter the future with a nonchalance likely to invite the perils much of the rest of urban America has endured.

Planning will be the most important issue of

Dallas's next decade. Whether planning is merely a superficial political exercise or turns out to be realistically ambitious will be determined by how the planning process is organized, how comprehensive it is, and how public involvement is enlisted.

Although Dallas city managers have tried for a long time to stimulate interest in planning by offering a variety of planning options (some of which were relatively radical in their call for increased local government regulation of the city's growth), successive city councils have been reluctant to plunge into planning.

This resistance stems in part from the unavoidable controversies that master planning generates. Battle lines inevitably would be drawn between the council and private developers. Some developers react violently to the prospect of tighter zoning ordinances and demands for increased contributions toward the street improvements and other services their projects necessitate.

The philosophy behind Dallas's tentative planning ideas is one of partnership — friendly if possible, imposed if not — between the public and private sectors.

According to this approach, gone are the days when growth could proceed willy-nilly, with the city government providing de facto support for private developers by meeting the growing demands for services (police, fire, sewage, etc.) created by this development.

The developers always claimed the city was not making any sacrifice; growth, they said, expanded the city's tax base and ensured widespread economic health.

That argument has its merits, but it also contains an element of basic unfairness. The city's taxpayers are compelled to indirectly subsidize private profit-making enterprises by helping pay for city services. Some projects, such as downtown office towers, are likely to generate tax revenues exceeding city costs, but other, more speculative ventures might never produce tax revenues equal to the city's services costs.

The alternative to Dallas's traditional laissez-faire approach is for the city council to enact much more rigid development guidelines to bar projects that will end up costing the city too much (for example, a development requiring extensive new sewer lines and roadwork but without the "gold mine" prospects likely to produce tax revenue).

Such an approach to planning would not be merely a matter of adjusting some statutes. It would, rather, be a substantial redefinition of the political philosophy that has stimulated Dallas's remarkably prosperous growth. That is why the city council has proceeded so cautiously whenever it is asked to consider planning issues.

Given the sweeping effects planning policies have, the process for developing these policies must be as democratic as possible. Developers, homeowners, elected officials, and anyone else interested in the city's future should be given an opportunity to be heard before the planning process moves too far along.

This will require yet another major change in the

way Dallas goes about its business. Although the doors to broad-based participation are open (at least to persons persistent enough to knock), most decisions still are made by a few elected officials, professional administrators, and business leaders (some of whom work through the Chamber of Commerce, Central Dallas Association, or Citizens' Council; many of whom wield influence on their own).

This base is not broad enough if Dallas's entire growth policy is to be revised. The magic formula most Dallas planners seek is one that both encourages and controls growth, a difficult balance to strike.

To a considerable extent, the seriousness of the city's planning efforts will be measured by the sophistication employed in creating the plan. Merely forcing some developers to foot the bill for street improvements or to limit the height of a few office buildings isn't planning. Instead, the city must carefully decide on its optimal look and "feel" for the coming decades; that is what planning is all about.

Planning the Dallas of the future is partly an exercise in mapmaking. Where should development be encouraged, and what kinds of development should occur in the various sectors of the city?

Some parts of town desperately need development, others already are overladen with construction that outpaces consumer demand and city services. For example, economically backward South Dallas has been virtually untouched by the Dallas boom, while parts of North Dallas (mainly north of LBJ Freeway) have seen so much building that traffic is perpetually snarled. North Dallas has become something of a city unto itself, but it has done so with all the thoughtful planning of the California gold rush.

A citywide master plan would encourage spreading out the affluence of growth, and it would reassure homeowners and other property owners (particularly those with small holdings) that they could plan for their futures without fears of their neighborhoods suddenly being drastically changed.

The most volatile planning issue to date has been that of neighborhood disruption. Dallas homeowners have been quite successful at blocking expanded highways and commercial development in or adjacent to residential areas. The need for constant vigilance about zoning matters has created a persistent tension between citizens and their local government. This lack of trust impairs the ability of the council and city boards to govern as effectively as they might. This probably will continue as long as some citywide political campaigns hinge on "developer-versus-homeowner" issues.

Community-based planning exercises (such as that somewhat successfully conducted in Oak Lawn), if orchestrated by a master planning staff at city hall, could do much both to alleviate the political tensions the absence of planning has exacerbated.

The planning process can't go so far that it drives development out of Dallas. Developers traditionally have at least implicitly threatened to move elsewhere if Dallas itself becomes too rigorous in its zoning and other planning requirements. Suburban communities such as Irving's Las Colinas avidly court businesses, offering a tantalizing location (between downtown Dallas and D/FW Airport) and less onerous regulation of growth.

This quest for corporate residents goes on continuously and sometimes is an underlying issue in seemingly unrelated matters. For example, a long-running political fight in Dallas has centered on noise pollution emanating from Love Field, the city's in-town airport. Anti-noise partisans have organized skillfully and have asked the city council to limit the airport's take-off and landing routes and its hours of operation. These activists offer convincing evidence of the disruption the noise causes in schools and the negative impact it has on residential property values.

Council sympathy for the anti-noise crusaders is, however, tempered by quiet reminders from businesses headquartered in downtown Dallas that they need a fully operational Love Field for quick access to Houston, Austin, and other cities served by airlines based there. The threat is clear: If deprived of this convenient air transportation, the businesses might have to move closer to D/FW Airport, which probably would mean moving outside Dallas's city limits.

Whether it be a question of air transportation or some other essential service, today's city always is hard-pressed to retain its attractiveness to its residents. Moving is so easy, and so many other communities are eager for new tax revenues, that the threat of corporate or residential flight is always present.

Such moves, if they happen on a large scale, can spell economic disaster for a city. If a corporation with its headquarters in Dallas moves to Irving, for example, it starts paying local taxes to Irving, not Dallas.

Erosion of the tax base is the quintessential urban crisis. If a pattern of corporate flight from the city is established, eventually you find the city populated mostly by those who can't afford to leave and also can't afford to provide the city with substantial tax revenues.

The tax base must be protected. That rule is the foundation for all planning. With that premise accepted, the task becomes finding ways to make the city work well enough to hold its current residents and attract new ones while steadily improving the city's quality of life.

In the effort to ensure proper delivery of services, Dallas's professional administrators are reconsidering the city's density patterns.

Dallas, unlike most large cities, always has had room to sprawl. Dallas's 900,000 residents occupy 378 square miles. This seems like vast space when compared to a city such as Washington, D.C., which has had roughly as many residents living in its 69 square miles.

Dallas has annexed some small contiguous communities, but much of the city's growth has occurred on what until recently had been clear acreage (once farmland) within the city limits. Even by the early 1980s, fields and wooded areas well within the city were being turned by developers into shopping centers, office buildings, and apartment complexes.

So far, the city government has done well in

keeping up with the demands for services this growth engenders. Wherever the new construction takes place, the city must provide police and fire protection, water hook-ups, street upkeep, and the other basics.

Property owners in Dallas have come to expect not only that these services be provided, but that they be of high quality. People are accustomed to having potholes filled promptly, without having to nag city hall.

Perhaps Dallas's citizens have been spoiled by the tradition of good service from their local government. But times are changing. If growth patterns in Dallas remain as they are, residents will have to make a choice: either pay steadily rising taxes to support the surging demand for services, or else scale back those services.

A compromise might be found. Fostering increased density of growth in certain locations, as opposed to letting new development pop up in scattered places throughout the city, would make it easier and less expensive for the city to provide services.

This policy raises major administrative and political questions. Where are the best locations to encourage concentrations of development and how can Dallas's services be better organized to support such clusters? The principal political issue again involves the implicit repudiation of laissez faire in favor of a more tightly managed approach to growth.

Is it worth it? By early 1984, despite city manager Charles Anderson's repeated urgings that the city council consider this different approach to managing the city's growth and resources, little thoughtful discussion had taken place among the persons who eventually would have to vote on ordinances that would make increased density a reality in Dallas.

An easier, less controversial route for the council would be to squeeze the city budget, trimming services gradually. Such council action is based on the political judgment that voters will favor holding the line on taxes even if doing so means sacrificing some quantity and quality in city services.

As a temporary measure, this judgment probably is correct. What council members haven't bothered to consider is what happens when the invisible line between acceptable and unacceptable service is crossed. If trash pickups become too infrequent or police response times too lengthy, will the voters demand improvement in such services, even if taxes must be raised?

The temptation to which most council members succumb is to defer answering such questions, hoping that a later city council will have to deal with these matters. The trade-off is dangerous: Refusal to increase taxes when demand and costs are increasing can work for a short time, but eventually compensating for such frugality will be expensive. Some future city council probably have to enact a substantial tax increase to bring the level of services back up to what the voters want.

On a related topic, the debate over density will accelerate because of Dallas's 1983 commitment to build a multi-billion dollar mass transit system.

Virtually every recent public opinion survey in Dallas has found transportation to be the number one issue on the minds of Dallas-area residents. In a city that never has known adequate public transit, most citizens have only a vague idea of what they want. They know, however, that things cannot continue as they are.

The private automobile reigns supreme in Dallas. Only one highway is a toll road. Parking in downtown still can be found for a few dollars per day. Bus service is relatively efficient, but has been severely limited, not even reaching some of the growing suburbs. When compared with low parking rates downtown, even the bus fares have seemed expensive. Given the limitations of Dallas's public transit system, most people do not see any reasonable (or necessary) alternative to driving their cars.

Yet by the early 1980s, demands grew louder for a sophisticated and comprehensive public transit system. The reason for the mounting outcry is visible any weekday during rush hour. Traffic on many major arteries doesn't move; it sits. Commuter frustration is proving to be the great motivator for the sweeping political and social changes inherent in creating a mass transit plan.

The pressure for transit improvements is not found in Dallas alone. Although Dallas proper, with 900,000 residents, certainly needs transit help, the increasingly extended limits of "greater Dallas" demand more efficient ways to move people over considerable distances. (Dallas County's population is 1.6 million; that of the overall Dallas-Fort Worth metropolitan area is about 3.2 million.) Some of the persons who work in downtown Dallas commute from homes beyond the reaches not only of the City of Dallas, but also those of Dallas County.

Playing "catch up" is expensive. Cost estimates for a combined bus and light rail system to be in place by the turn of the century run at about $2 billion. Principal funding will come from rider fares and a locally imposed sales tax, with some state and federal aid.

Creation of a governing body responsible for transit always has been viewed warily by most voters. Such a body would levy taxes and plan sweeping projects that would have substantial impact on property values, the environment, and virtually every other aspect of community life. When presented with a proposal to create a Lone Star Transit Authority (LSTA) for the Dallas area in 1980, voters said "no," defeating the referendum measure by a substantial margin.

Reasons for this election outcome were more political than transit-related. The pro-LSTA campaign was run on a small budget and met vocal opposition from neighborhood activists, who argued that too great a danger existed that the transit authority would create routes without considering impact on residents, particularly in neighborhoods close to downtown. LSTA boosters were unable to articulate either the need for their plan or the specific goals of that plan.

The failure of the LSTA measure turned out to be helpful because it forced people to look more closely at transit plans. Mass transit proponents realized they must create not only a technical proposal concentrating on routes, fares, and different modes of transit, but also, on a larger scale, they must develop a more comprehensive understanding of what transit means to a community.

In preparing for the 1983 transit referendum, planners of the Dallas Area Rapid Transit (DART) board were careful not to repeat the political negligence that was a cause of the 1980 transit referendum defeat.. They spent over $1 million on a professionally managed campaign and sold the idea of mass transit as if it was a candidate for office. They stressed that Dallas could no longer put off work on a transit system; further postponement would ensure Houston-like traffic chaos.

These arguments worked. The DART proposal passed by a comfortable margin in Dallas, and 13 out of the 20 suburban cities that voted on the measure agreed to join the system.

A principal reason for DART's electoral success was that its proponents were able to articulate convincing arguments about the city's general need for mass transit. Such a philosophy of transportation is essential given the ramifications of implementing any kind of transit system. The impact on the individual's lifestyle can be profound when he is presented with new ways to get from place to place and is told that his old habits should (or must) change.

Weaning people from their cars isn't easy. If the public does not accept the basic notion that mass transit is essential, no plan, however well-intentioned and carefully crafted, is worth the effort or cost that goes into it.

The symbiotic relationship between planning and overall city growth is something Dallas has only slowly begun to recognize. The politics of transit has involved not merely convincing people of the need for carefully considered, specific transportation modes and routes, but also reassuring voters that transit governance will not be conducted by an oppressive, unduly costly, and unaccountable technocracy.

Added to these political measures is the density issue. Some Dallas planners envision DART as not merely a way of moving people, but also a way to create a blueprint for growth. New apartment buildings, office complexes, and retail malls (and the support services they require) should, according to density theorists, be attracted to DART's rail and bus lines.

However accurate the planners' theses turn out to be, the future of the city depends largely on less scientific judgments that will be made by residents. Why live in Dallas, particularly as opposed to the suburbs? What aspects of Dallas life should be maintained as they are? What should be added or improved?

The responsiveness of the city government will influence answers to such questions. Elected officials and administrators at city hall proudly point to "public input" opportunities that are provided at weekly council meetings and as part of individual projects, such as revision of zoning ordinances.

Although the motivations behind such efforts are, for the most part, sincere, the process itself often turns out to be window dressing. The roster of speakers at council meetings usually contains many of the same names week after week, and most of these persons represent no one except themselves.

Similarly, efforts to solicit citizens' views about specific city policies are handled in haphazard ways. If useful representative opinions are provided, that usually is because neighborhood organizations or other interest groups have galvanized their memberships to lobby the decision-makers.

If city officials are sincere about wanting to further democratize Dallas's governance, they need to create mechanisms to regularly reach a broad-based constituency. Of course, not everyone wants to participate in city affairs; many prefer to trust the government to work on its own. But Dallas will make a substantive contribution to the processes of urban government only if it finds ways to foster more activism.

Some city council meetings could be scheduled outside city hall (in community centers, for example). The city manager, police chief, and other professionals could regularly schedule hearings on current issues in the individual council districts. The city could more frequently organize planning forums that bring together residents and developers, thus avoiding some needless conflicts.

The unquestionably efficient administration of Dallas's government does not justify increasing distance between governors and governed. Remoteness is a symptom of smugness, which in turn is a political trait that voters are likely to eventually strip away. Pre-emptive efforts to democratize the city's governance could make such traumatic polarization unnecessary.

This more expansive approach to governance would be tested early in the increasingly restive residential neighborhoods. Extensive debate is needed about the whole notion of what might be called urban protectionism — the designation of certain residential zones as areas in which commercial development will not be allowed to intrude.

This issue is politically volatile because in many cases it will involve backzoning (which downgrades the level of development allowed) to correct the overly flexible zoning that might allow incompatible uses within an area.

Backzoning often evokes screams of anguish from developers who have purchased land based on what the original zoning indicated would be permissible development. If backzoning is to occur, it should be initiated promptly. Uncertainty about planning and zoning can depress real estate values and discourage even the most responsible developer.

Dallas is trying to walk the narrow line between controlled growth and no growth, recognizing that the former is difficult to define, but that the latter could be ruinous economically. The emerging political power of neighborhood groups makes this path even more tortuous. Although these organizations share some common philosophies, each neighborhood has some unique interests that are paramount.

Some politicians might seize upon these differences as a way to divide and conquer, pitting different neighborhoods against each other. This kind of Balkanization could cripple the effectiveness of the loud (but not always coherent) voices of neighborhood activists.

To avoid this will require political organizing that is more sophisticated and more persistent than any the neighborhoods have yet undertaken. We are soon likely to see what amounts to a neighborhood political party that endorses, works for, and contributes funds to candidates. This in turn will perpetuate the homeowner-versus-developer struggle.

Much bitterness could arise from such politicking. Before all the parties involved are locked into stringently adversary positions, the city hall leadership could act to defuse tensions. This will require increased openness in the city's planning process, but, more important, it will require more formal recognition of the importance and power of neighborhoods in shaping the city's future.

Closely tied to the future of Dallas's neighborhoods are the prospects for the city's public education system. In addition to teacher competency, availability of classrooms, and other frequently discussed issues, a psychological obstacle must be considered when trying to determine whether the public schools will survive.

The 1985 school bond election victory provided almost $200 million in essential bricks-and-mortar money. The voter support reflected in this campaign's results needs nurturing if it is to become the foundation of a continuing commitment to upgrade the DISD.

Many people have become convinced that the

public schools can't work and have predicted their imminent demise. Such prophecies can become self-fulfilling.

Dallas has yet to decide if it *wants* public education to continue. Although student performance has improved and the administration of the system has become more professional, parents remain skeptical about the DISD's ability to create the desired product: properly educated children.

Parent organizations dedicated to revitalizing the schools have improved the DISD's prospects. But all the good will in the world is not enough to save the schools. Massive transfusions of money are essential.

The state legislature has committed substantial new funding to public education, but the competition for state tax dollars is fierce and the legislature's steadfastness is questionable. The federal government is rapidly moving out of the education business. The burden, therefore, rests squarely on the local community.

Diverse ways to secure funds must be found for everything from teacher pay to textbook purchases to capital improvements. Local school district taxes will be the cornerstone, but the basic school tax rate cannot be raised so high that it precipitates a taxpayer revolt. Supplemental tax money might be generated by, for example, a local "sin tax" on liquor and tobacco (assuming the state legislature will authorize such). Also, private sector aid from foundations and businesses must be more actively solicited.

It is too late for halfway measures. The message in all these fund-raising initiatives must be: If you want public education in Dallas, put your money where your mouth is.

Particularly when compared with the status of the public schools, the prospects for the arts in Dallas look good. The major institutions such as the Dallas Museum of Art are likely to enjoy increasing public support and stable financial futures.

Even these large, wealthy institutions will remain somewhat vulnerable since their destinies are partly controlled by the city council. The arts entities cannot let down their political guard; budget-cutting council members will pounce on any organization they think lacks political resilience.

The principal test for Dallas arts will center on the survival skills of smaller arts organizations and individual artists. Aiding these enterprising groups and individuals might not be as fashionable as contributing to the museum or symphony, but artistic growth in the city will be stunted without a diverse, lively population in this less ostentatious arts community.

Another task for Dallas's arts leaders will be to expand the constituency of arts supporters. No longer may a museum simply secure an exhibition, hang it on its walls, and wait for people to come to see it.

Cultural missionary work must be carried on, educating people about the arts and stimulating as many persons as possible — from kindergarten student to senior citizen — to contemplate the beauty and genius inherent in works of art.

Dallas will become a major arts center only when this kind of interest in the arts becomes more widely accepted as an integral part of the city's daily life.

As with the arts, the availability of health care in Dallas is poised on the brink of excellence. The quality of care continues to improve, particularly that offered by Parkland Hospital to the community's indigents.

Delivery of care, however, does not match this quality. Too much of the area's population remains medically underserved. The health of people who for whatever reason do not receive care remains unconscionably susceptible to problems that could be cured. It is as if these persons were living in an earlier century or in some remote outpost.

Providing health care (including mental health services) to an ever-expanding constituency requires massive expenditures. As with public education, this process won't work unless the people decide they want it to.

The average premature baby in Parkland Hospital requires care costing between $20,000 and $60,000. Someone must pay the bill. So far, Dallas taxpayers have done this, but will they not only keep paying the present rate but also agree to pay more so everyone who needs care can receive it?

Again, the taxpayer should not be expected to shoulder the entire burden. Private aid to medical facilities in Dallas always has been extraordinarily generous; it must become even more so. The alternative (which could be faced soon) is to deny care to some of those who need it.

In most of these matters, the poor are those most likely to be shut out. Perhaps the most difficult task for the Dallasite contemplating his city's future is to lower his line of vision from the lofty premise the downtown skyline holds and look more closely at those who have been passed by in the city's rush to affluence.

No miracles will occur. No formula exists that will transform the slums near Fair Park into neat and prosperous neighborhoods such as those in North Dallas. No instant enlightenment will dispel the racism that runs as an undercurrent throughout much of Dallas's social and political life.

The only way to address these problems is to admit that they exist and to understand that they can be solved solely through long and hard work. The "can do" spirit in which Dallas takes so much pride will be sorely tested, but by creatively stimulating economic development (and thus increasing jobs and benefits) in the neediest parts of the city, Dallas might yet become a true model of urban prosperity.

AFTERWORD: THE CITY AND THE DREAM

The most realistic prognosis for Dallas is one based on cautious optimism.

Reasons both tangible and intangible shape this outlook. Fiscal indicators remain strong. Dallas's economy has not become overly dependent on any single kind of business such as the reliance on the oil industry that brought first feast and then famine to some Texas cities. The employment rate is good, suffering only during the occasional onslaughts of job-seekers from elsewhere in the country. Consumer spending outpaces the national rate. Long-term residential and business construction patterns indicate the boomtown will continue to boom.

How will the wealth this growth generates affect the city as a whole? Some people undoubtedly will become very rich, but will prosperity touch the lives of the persons who so far have not enjoyed the benefits of Dallas's healthy economy? Will a large enough share of profits reach the city's coffers to help ensure responsive, effective governance?

These are the kinds of questions Dallas has yet to thoughtfully ponder, much less answer.

Beyond the need to define further the general philosophy of the city, many specific issues require more attention than they have yet received. Some of these might not seem of great consequence at the moment, but they will profoundly affect the Dallas of the future.

For example, will homeowners be assured that traffic routing will not take precedence over the habitability of residential neighborhoods? Given the diminishing amounts of federal and state aid, will the city and county governments continue to ensure adequate health care, education, and other basic services, especially to persons who can't pay for them? To what extent will the green space needed to let the city breathe be preserved in the face of continuing development?

Dallas's youthfulness, relative to the ages of many other American cities, has its good and bad sides. Even if the vibrant confidence of a young city on the rise remains intact, it can be accompanied by inexperience that will impair responses to many of the questions, such as those mentioned here, that other cities already have been forced to answer.

Coupled with this limited experience, the absence of serious adversity has meant that Dallas has not had to develop the rigorous self-discipline that will become ever more essential in matters such as devising budgets and long-range plans.

As Dallas chases its future, hopefulness and good intentions abound. Dallas assumes it will grow and prosper, but it has yet to decide what kind of city it wants to be.

Only when the people of Dallas more seriously address this question, will Dallas have a good chance to fully realize the urban dream.

APPENDIX

Source for Appendix data: Dallas Chamber of Commerce.

CITY OF DALLAS

Population 1983	938,250
Number of households	379,200
Female	51.9%
White	61.4%
Spanish surname	12.3%
Black	29.4%
Other	9.2%
Age 18-24	14.5%
Age 25-34	19.9%
Age 35-49	16.8%
Age 50 and older	23.2%
College graduate (or more)	22.0%
Population change, 1970-1980	+7.1%
Population change, 1980-1983	+3.7%
U.S. population ranking 1983	7

DALLAS AREA RAPID TRANSIT (DART)

(Service to be implemented by 1986)

Type of Bus Service	Route Miles
Local	1,391
Express	170
Crosstown	247
Subscription	62
Total	1,870

Bus service to be increased in City of Dallas by 35%.

DART Rail Component

69 miles by 1995
131 miles by 2000
160 miles by 2010
98 transit stations

Cities to be served by DART

Addison
Carrollton
Cockrell Hill
Coppell
Dallas
Farmers Branch
Flower Mound
Garland
Glenn Heights
Highland Park
Irving
Plano
Richardson
Rowlett
University Park

DALLAS INDEPENDENT SCHOOL DISTRICT, 1983

Total enrollment	127,462
Teacher/Pupil Ratios:	
Kindergarten	1/25
First Grade	1/22
Second and Third Grades	1/24
Fourth through Sixth Grades	1/27
Seventh & Eighth Grades	1/25
Ninth through Twelfth Grades	1/25
Total Number of Schools:	
Elementary (K-6)	129
Middle Schools (7-8)	23
High Schools (9-12)	20
Magnet Schools	6
Alternative Schools	5
Total	183

OTHER SCHOOLS, 1983

Private and Parochial (Accredited)	37
Colleges & Universities (within 100 miles of Dallas):	
4 year	26
2 year	19
Technical-Vocational Schools (Dallas-Fort Worth)	75
Health Related	4

LABOR FORCE STATISTICS, 1983 (Thousands)

	City of Dallas	Dallas-Ft. Worth SMSA
Total Labor Force	552.8	1,819.2
Employed	525.0	1,737.4
Unemployed	27.8	81.8
Unemployment Rate	5.0%	4.5%

HOSPITAL BEDS, DALLAS COUNTY, 1983-1984 9,499

CRIME RATE PER 1,000 POPULATION, CITY OF DALLAS, 1983

	1983	1982	% Change ('82-83)
Aggravated Assault	5.86	6.49	-9.7
Murder	0.29	0.33	-12.1
Rape	0.97	1.21	-19.8
Robbery	5.31	6.22	-14.6
Auto Theft	7.95	7.88	+0.9
Burglary	32.01	36.38	-12.0
Larceny	64.56	67.99	-5.0
Total	116.95	126.50	-7.5%

CITY OF DALLAS SERVICES, 1983

Police stations	5
Police Department uniformed strength	2,109
Fire stations	50
Fire Department uniformed strength	1,595
Park sites	281
Park acreage	19,289
Public Library branches	19
Public Library holdings	4,133,630
18-hole golf courses	6
Tennis centers	5
Swimming pools	107

TOTAL VALUATION OF BUILDING PERMITS, CITY OF DALLAS

1982	$1,552,924,860
1983	$1,792,111,698

HOUSING STARTS, 1983

	1983	1982
City of Dallas		
Single-Family	3,264	2,283
Avg. New House Value	$133,600	$132,000
Multi-Family Units	19,219	9,613
Total Units	22,483	11,896
Dallas-PMSA		
Single-family	19,694	10,945
Avg. New House Value	$93,300	$92,400
Multi-Family Units	55,971	28,346
Total Units	75,665	39,291

Office Space Square Footage, Dallas Metropolitan Area

Jan. 1984 Status	Total Square Feet
Existing	77,868,024
Under Construction	14,367,501
Proposed/Planned	14,134,497

CITY GOVERNMENT FINANCES, 1983-1984 *(Approved Budget)*

Revenues	
General Government Revenues	$394,689,955
Enterprise Fund Revenues	$236,069,830
Debt Service Fund Revenues	$66,846,000
Deferred Maintenance Fund Revenues	$4,339,529
Total Revenues	$701,945,314
Percentage of General Government Revenues, By Sources	
Federal and State Government	1.0%
Property Taxes	38.5%
General Sales Taxes	22.7%
Charges, User Fees	10.4%
Other Sources	27.4%
Per Capita General Government Revenues	$420.67
Expenditures	
General Government Expenditures	$394,689,955
Enterprise Fund Expenditures	$232,330,281
Debt Service Expenditures	$66,846,000
Deferred Maintenance Expenditures	$4,339,529
Total Expenditures	$698,205,765
Per Capita General Government Expenditures	$420.67
Fire and Police	$190.19
Streets and Sanitation	$56.54
Parks and Libraries	$53.98
Building Services	$19.87
Health and Human Services	$10.25
Public Works	$8.27

INDEX

ABOUT THE PHOTOGRAPHER

Daniel Barsotti was born in Memphis, Tennessee and is a 1973 graduate of Southern Methodist University. He makes his home in Dallas, Texas and has won numerous awards for his photography. Exhibitions of his work include "Emerging Texas Photography, 1980", the Dallas Museum of Art, and "Art and the Law." He served on the faculty of The University of Texas Medical School at Dallas in the Medical Arts Department and owns his own freelance studio. He has served as the Artist in Residence for the City of Dallas.